THE TOTAL FUNK BASSIST

>> A Fun and Comprehensive Overview of Funk Bass Playing

DAVE OVERTHROW

Alfred Music
P.O. Box 10003
Van Nuys, CA 91410-0003
alfred.com

ISBN-10: 0-7390-6014-7 (Book & CD)
ISBN-13: 978-0-7390-6014-8 (Book & CD)

CD recorded and mastered by Collin Tilton at Bar None Studio, Northford, CT
Dave Overthrow (bass), Kurt Berglund (drums), Mark Garthwait (guitar), Brian Leary (keyboard)

Interior photography by Timothy Phelps, Dave Overthrow, and Yvette Overthrow

Cover Photographs
Funky Bassist: © Joseph C. Justice Jr. / iStockphoto.com • Bass on cover courtesy Schecter Guitar Research

Contents

About the Author

Dave Overthrow has performed throughout the United States and Europe with a wide variety of jazz, funk, and rock artists, including his own Dave Overthrow Band. His work has led him to performances with Stanley Clark, Mike Stern, Frank Gambale, Trey Anastasio, John Abercrombie, Sonny Landreth, Aaron Scott, Ken Gioffre, and Nick Bariluk.

Dave served a three-year stint as a staff writer for *Bass Guitar Magazine* and has written numerous instructional books for electric bass (all published by Alfred). He has also filmed three instructional DVDs and 60 online video lessons for WorkshopLive.com.

Dave taught bass seminars at various campuses for the National Guitar Workshop (where he taught since 1983) and was the Director of Music and Chair of Jazz Studies at the Canterbury School in New Milford, CT.

The Dave Overthrow Band has released two CDs: *In the Pocket* and *2 Hot to Touch*. Dave plays SWR amplifiers, Ron Blake Custom Basses, and DR Handmade Strings.

Other Titles by Dave Overthrow

Beginning Electric Bass
(Book and CD; Alfred #19362)
(DVD; Alfred #22889)
Intermediate Electric Bass
(Book and CD; Alfred #19359)
Mastering Electric Bass
(Book and CD; Alfred #19356)
30-Day Bass Workout
(Book; Alfred #20398)
(DVD; Alfred #24211)
Slap & Pop Bass
(Book and CD; Alfred #21904)
Beginning Blues Bass
(Book and CD; Alfred #22591)
(DVD; Alfred #24416)
Beginning Bass For Adults
(Book and CD; #07-1085)
The Total Jazz Bassist
(Book and CD; Alfred #26063)

Acknowledgements

Thanks to everyone at NGW, Workshop Arts, SWR, DR Strings; and to Ron Blake for the great basses. Thanks to the following for playing on the CD that accompanies this book: Brian Leary (keyboard), Mark Garthwait (guitar), and Kurt Berglund (drums).

Thanks to all of the musicians I have played with in my musical journey.

Thanks to Yvette for her love, patience, and support.

Introduction

Welcome, fellow funksters. Funk is one of the most exciting genres of music to play on the bass. The foundation of all funk music is the groove, and the groove is laid down primarily by the bassist and the drummer. Funk is not a cerebral music, but rather, a genre that compels you to move your hips, tap your feet, bob your head, and get up and get down.

There are several artists who were instrumental in the development of funk music. The "Godfather of Soul," James Brown, was a major force in soul and R&B throughout the 1950s and '60s, and those two genres would later evolve into what is now known as funk. In the early 1970s, two groups were responsible for the birth of funk as its own genre: Parliament-Funkadelic and Graham Central Station.

Funk music has evolved over the years and has spawned a new generation of funk bassists. Along with the music, bass technique has evolved as well. The slap & pop style introduced by Larry Graham has developed over the years, and bassists continue adding to the technique. Funk has fused with other genres, and its influence can be seen in rock, reggae, jazz, and other styles. From Larry Graham, Bootsy Collins, Flea, and Stanley Clarke to the wizardry of Marcus Miller and Victor Wooten, the slap & pop style has become an integral part of funk bass playing.

Even though slap & pop has become so essential to funk, many classic funk tunes featured the fingerstyle funk technique. Two of the funkiest bassists of all time used this technique exclusively: Jaco Pastorius and Rocco Prestia. Jaco and Rocco are responsible for some of the funkiest bass grooves ever recorded, without ever slapping or popping a note!

This book discusses the various techniques used in funk bass playing, including fingerstyle funk, muting, slap & pop, hammer-ons, pull-offs, popped double stops, double thumping, and double popping. There are hundreds of funk bass grooves at a variety of playing levels. Each chapter progresses in a concise, logical manner, taking you from beginning fingerstyle and slap & pop bass all the way to advanced techniques like double popping and double thumping. To get the most out of this book, you should have some experience reading standard music notation or TAB and be comfortable with basic playing technique. However, for beginners and those of you who would like a refresher, a review of these concepts can be found starting on page 6.

The goal of this book is to teach you how to lock into the funk groove (otherwise known as playing "in the pocket"). And if you can get people moving while playing some great funk bass grooves, that's cool too. Enjoy!

0

Track 1

A compact disc is available with this book. Using the disc will help make learning more enjoyable and the information more meaningful. Listening to the CD will help you correctly interpret the rhythms and feel of each example. The symbol to the left appears next to each song or example that is performed on the CD. Example numbers are above the symbol. The track number corresponds directly to the song or example you want to hear. In some cases, there is more than one example per track; this is reflected in the track numbers (for example: Track 2.1, Track 2.2, Track 2.3, etc.). Track 1 will help you tune to this CD.

Chapter 1: Getting Started

Strings on the Bass

To the right is a diagram showing the four strings on the bass. The 4th string (E) is the thickest string and is closest to the ceiling when playing. The 1st string (G) is the thinnest string and is closest to the floor when playing. The diagram also shows the notes of the *musical alphabet* (A–B–C–D–E–F–G) on the fretboard.

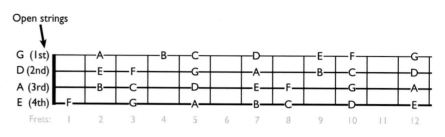

Tuning

There are different methods for tuning your bass. The easiest and most practical method for beginning players is to use an *electronic tuner*. Since it takes time to develop a musical ear and identify the exactness of pitch, using the tuner is the easiest way to tune your instrument. It tells you whether or not your instrument is in tune. If your string is *flat* (too low), tighten the tuning peg to raise the pitch. If the string is *sharp* (too high), loosen the tuning peg to lower the pitch.

There are two main types of electronic tuners. The first type automatically senses which pitch you are playing. The second type requires you to set a dial, or knob, to your target pitch. Whichever type of tuner you use, you will need to make sure you are actually tuning to the correct pitch. For example, your 1st string may be so flat that the tuner senses it as an F♯ instead of a G. In this case, turn the tuning peg to tighten the string. At first, it will show up as a sharp F♯, but then as you tighten the string, the tuner will register it as a flat G, and then an in-tune G. Make sure you don't miss your target note and tune the string all the way up to A♭.

Relative Tuning

You can also tune your bass by ear. If you can hear the difference in pitches well, you can try to tune this way. Beginning players might need to develop their ears a little more before they can use this method.

To the right is an easy process for getting in tune without the help of an electronic tuner. (Also, see illustration at the bottom of page.)

Step 1) Tune your open 4th string (E) to a piano, keyboard, pitch pipe, or other instrument of constant pitch (meaning, it doesn't have to be tuned every time it is played). On a keyboard, use the E that is 19 white keys below middle C (see diagram below).

Step 2) To tune your 3rd string, place a finger on the 5th fret of the 4th string to produce the note A. The open 3rd string should match this note. If not, use the tuning peg for the 3rd string to adjust it up (if the string is flat) or down (if the string is sharp).

Step 3) To tune your 2nd string, place a finger on the 5th fret of the 3rd string to produce the note D. The open 2nd string should match this note. If not, use the tuning peg for the 2nd string to adjust it up (if the string is flat) or down (if the string is sharp).

Step 4) To tune your 1st string, place a finger on the 5th fret of the 2nd string to produce the note G. The open 1st string should match this note. If not, use the tuning peg for the 1st string to adjust it up (if the string is flat) or down (if the string is sharp).

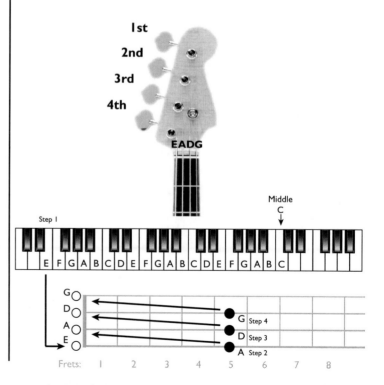

Standard Music Notation

Pitch

Pitch refers to the highness or lowness of musical sounds called *notes*. Pitch is indicated by placing notes on a *staff*. Notes appear in various ways. Every note has a *head*, and some have *stems* and *flags*. (See illustration to the right.)

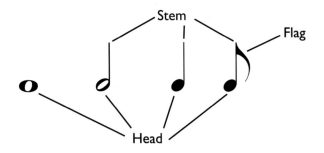

The Staff and Clef

The staff has five lines and four spaces and is read from left to right. At the beginning of the staff is a *clef*. The clef indicates what note corresponds to a particular line or space on the staff. Bass music is written in *bass clef* 𝄢, sometimes called *F clef*. The dots surround the F line.

Notes on the Staff

A good way to learn the notes on the staff is to memorize the letter names of the lines separately from the spaces. The note names are shown below, starting from the bottom line and then the bottom space. To help you memorize them, a catchy phrase is suggested for each group of notes.

Bass clef line names: **G–B–D–F–A**
(**G**ood **B**oys **D**o **F**ine **A**lways)

Bass clef space names: **A–C–E–G**
(**A**ll **C**ows **E**at **G**rass)

Notes on the lines: Notes on the spaces:

Ledger Lines

Lines that are located above or below the staff are called *ledger lines* (sometimes spelled *leger*). They are extensions of the staff and are used for notes that are too high, or too low, to be accommodated within the staff.

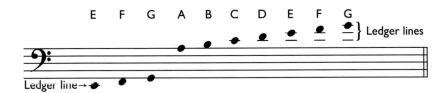

Accidentals

Accidentals are symbols that alter the pitch of a note.

♯ = *Sharp* sign. When this sign is to the left of a note, raise the note by one *half step* (one fret). For example, the note A is located on the 5th fret of the 4th string, so A♯ (A-sharp) is located on the 6th fret. When a note is sharped, it remains sharped for that entire *measure* (see next page).

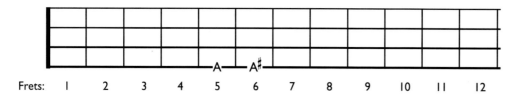

♭ = *Flat* sign. When this sign is to the left of a note, lower the note by one half step. For example, the note A is located on the 5th fret of the 4th string, so A♭ (A-flat) is located on the 4th fret. When a note is flatted, it remains flatted for that entire measure.

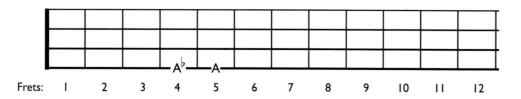

♮ = *Natural* sign. All notes without sharps or flats are considered to be *natural* notes. This symbol is used to indicate the change from a previously sharped or flatted note to the natural pitch. In other words, it cancels a previous sharp or flat.

✕ = *Double sharp* sign. When this sign is to the left of a note, raise the note by one *whole step* (two half steps, or two frets). For example, the note A is located on the 5th fret of the 4th string, so A✕ (A-double sharp) is located on the 7th fret. As with all accidentals, the double sharp remains in effect for the rest of the measure.

♭♭ = *Double flat* sign. When this sign is to the left of a note, lower the note by one whole step. For example, the note A is located on the 5th fret of the 4th string, so A♭♭ (A-double flat) is located on the 3rd fret. When a note is double-flatted, it remains double-flatted for that entire measure.

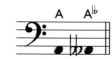

Time

Beats and Measures

Measures (also known as *bars*) divide music into groups of *beats*. A beat is a basic unit of time that can be thought of as the "pulse," or "heartbeat," of the music. The vertical lines that cross through the staff are called *barlines,* and they show where one measure begins and another ends. *Double barlines* mark the end of a section or small example. *Final barlines* end a song or longer example.

Note Durations

As you know, the location of a note in relation to the staff tells us its pitch (how high or low it is). The *duration,* or *value,* is indicated by its shape and stem.

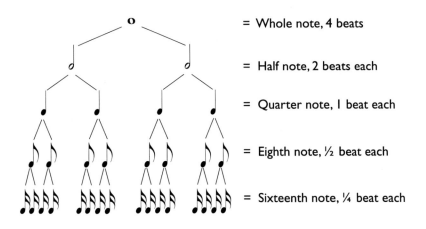

= Whole note, 4 beats

= Half note, 2 beats each

= Quarter note, 1 beat each

= Eighth note, ½ beat each

= Sixteenth note, ¼ beat each

Rests

So far, we've covered five types of note values. They each have a corresponding duration of silence known as a *rest.* A *whole rest* means four beats of silence, a *half rest* means two beats of silence, and so forth.

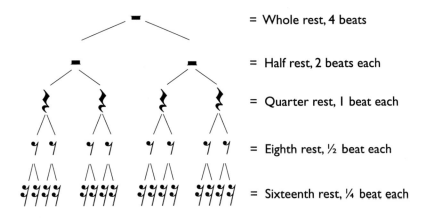

= Whole rest, 4 beats

= Half rest, 2 beats each

= Quarter rest, 1 beat each

= Eighth rest, ½ beat each

= Sixteenth rest, ¼ beat each

Time Signatures

At the beginning of any piece or song, you'll find a *time signature*. A time signature consists of two numbers, one on top of the other, and looks like a fraction. The top number indicates how many beats are in each measure. The bottom number tells you what kind of note gets one beat, and that number is usually a four, representing the quarter note.

$\frac{4}{4}$ 4 beats per measure
Quarter note ♩ = one beat

$\frac{3}{4}$ 3 beats per measure
Quarter note ♩ = one beat

$\frac{12}{8}$ 12 beats per measure
Eighth note ♪ = one beat

The time signature you'll encounter most frequently is $\frac{4}{4}$. For this reason, it is often called *common time* and is sometimes indicated with a **C**.

Dots and Ties

Sometimes, a note's duration cannot be expressed using a single rhythmic value. Instances of this include notes lasting for 3 beats or 1½ beats. In cases like these, a *dot* is placed directly to the right of the notehead. Dotted notes ring out 50% longer than their undotted versions. A dotted half note lasts three beats, a dotted quarter note lasts 1½ beats, and so forth (see right).

A *tie* is a curved line that connects two (or more) notes together. The result is the full duration of both tied notes. For example, a half note tied to a quarter note should sustain for three beats.

Triplets

Triplets consist of three notes in the time of two. For example, one eighth-note triplet equals one beat (three eighth notes instead of two). It would take four eighth-note triplets to fill a measure in $\frac{4}{4}$.

Eighth-note triplets

Swing Eighths

Most funk music is played with a straight eight-note feel. However, sometimes it is played using *swing eighths*. This rhythm is notated differently than it sounds. Swing eighths are written as regular eighth notes, but in performance, the first eighth note is longer than the second, almost like a triplet with the first two eighth notes tied (♫ = ♫). In this book, all examples using swing eighths are indicated by the symbol *Swing 8ths*.

Bass Tablature (TAB)

Tablature, or *TAB*, is used to indicate where notes are located on the fretboard of the bass. TAB was used well before music for fretted instruments was written in standard music notation (prior to 1800).

This is how TAB works. The four lines represent the four strings of the bass; the top line is the 1st string (G). The numbers on the lines tell you which frets to play. Numbers beneath the TAB staff tell you which left-hand fingers to use (the fingers of the left hand are numbered 1–4 starting with the index finger, see diagram to the right). Modern TAB will often include the notes in standard music notation above it (see example below).

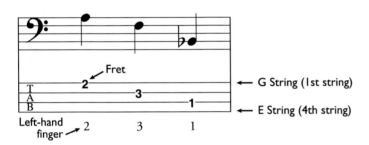

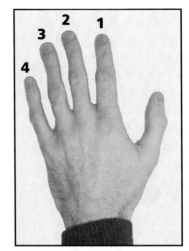

Fingers of the left hand.

In the example above, the number 2 is on the top line, so the note is located on the 2nd fret of the 1st string. The number 3 is on the 2nd line, so this note is played on the 3rd fret of the 2nd string. The number 1 is located on the 3rd line, so this note is played on the 1st fret of the 3rd string.

Chord Symbols

A *chord* is three or more notes played simultaneously. Chords are indicated by *chord symbols* above the staff. Even though the bass player usually only plays one note at a time (leaving the full chord to the guitarist or other musicians), the notes you choose for your bass line must "fit" with the chords. That's why this book will show chord symbols above most music examples. They will help you understand the note choices in the bass lines and help you choose the notes for your own bass lines.

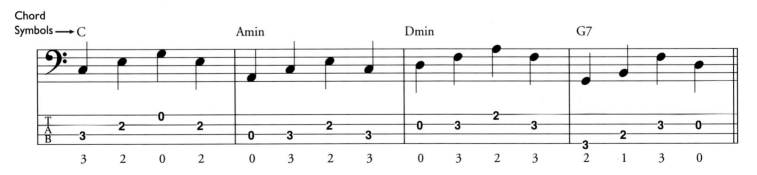

Basic Technique

Right-Hand Technique

It is common to play the electric bass in either the sitting or standing position. Whether you are playing sitting or standing, your bass should remain in the same position and angle, so the right- and left-hand techniques used for playing the instrument remain the same. Let's first examine right-hand technique.

Most bass players use the index finger, or 1st finger, to pluck the strings. Eventually, you will also use the middle, or 2nd, finger. Most bassists use a combination of the two and alternate their 1st and 2nd fingers to play the bass. Funk bassists also use the thumb to strike the strings (see page 77).

A commonly used technique is the *rest stroke*, where the finger plucks the string and comes to rest gently against the adjacent string. For example, the 1st finger plucks the 1st string, then rests against the 2nd string. This mutes the 2nd string, preventing unwanted notes from ringing out, and encourages efficient finger movement.

Thumb Position

The thumb can be anchored on the pickup when playing the 4th string (E).

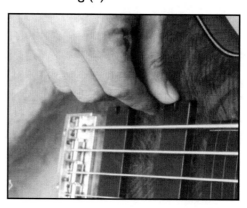

It can rest on the 4th string when playing the 3rd, 2nd, or 1st strings.

Left-Hand Technique

When holding the electric bass, place your left-hand thumb flat on the back of the neck, directly behind the 2nd finger. The thumb should mirror the movement of the 2nd finger when moving up and down the neck. The wrist is slightly arched to allow the fingers to curve naturally. The fingers should be as close to the frets as possible (just to the left) when pressing the strings.

The proper left-hand position is shown in the picture to the right.

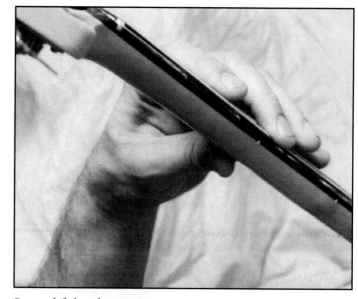

Proper left-hand position.

Chapter 2: Funk 101

What Is Funk?

What is funk? Have you ever heard a piece of music that affected you in a way that no other has? You couldn't help but gravitate towards this music? Your body couldn't resist the pulsating groove of the heavy bass interlocking with the drums? The rhythm section churns out rhythms with the power of a locomotive gaining speed with no signs of letting up? If you have heard such music, you have probably experienced funk.

To put it plain and simple, funk music is all about the groove. The groove is the key component to funk, and it is the bass, along with the drums, that is responsible for creating this groove. Funk is a blending of soul, jazz, and R&B into a rhythmic, danceable form of music that brings electric bass and drums to the foreground like no other music genre. Other instruments used to fill out a funk band are electric guitar, Hammond organ, and a horn section of saxes, trumpets, and, perhaps, a trombone.

Funk Masters

For examples of how "bad" funk bass can be, check out the music of the following funk masters: Bootsy Collins, Larry Graham, Louis Johnson, George Porter, Jr., Rocco Prestia, Flea, Marcus Miller, and Victor Wooten. For inspiration while working with this book, listen to their recordings and check out clips of them playing on YouTube.

Characteristics

The bass can be thought of as the centerpiece of a funk tune. The groove played by the bass is often as memorable as the melody and/or lyrics. The drums are also important and commonly play syncopated sixteenth-note rhythms that get the listener up and dancing rather than sitting there thinking about how wonderful the music is. Funk is a celebration of music, and there is no time to be inhibited about laying down a "fat" groove that people can dig. The emphasis is not how many hip notes you play, but what you do with each of these notes and how much passion you infuse in them. The test of a funk bass player is whether or not you can get the people moving and having a good time.

We are going to start our funk journey on the next page by looking at the most important aspect of funk (and probably all music): rhythm. Then we'll get into some fun funk techniques.

Note: A *metronome* is a device that keeps a steady beat and can be adjusted from slow to fast. Most of the examples in this book have *metronome markings*. The metronome marking indicates the *tempo*, or speed, of the music and designates how many beats can be played per minute. For example, ♩ = 120 indicates there are 120 quarter-note beats per minute. Therefore, when practicing, set your metronome to 120.

It is very important to practice with a metronome, *drum machine* (an electronic device that simulates drum sounds and can be set to play various rhythms at different speeds), or some other sort of time-keeping device. This will help you master the bass lines in this book more effectively. In addition, play along with the CD that accompanies this book and, whenever you can, practice with a drummer. Nothing can take the place of playing with a good drummer.

Sixteenth-Note Rhythm Studies

Funk bass lines often consist of sixteenth notes. Before you start playing sixteenth notes, it's important to know how to count quarter notes and eighth notes. Quarter notes are one beat each and are counted: 1, 2, 3, 4; 1, 2, 3, 4, etc. Eighth notes are one half of a beat each and are counted: 1–&, 2–&, 3–&, 4–&; 1–&, 2–&, 3–&, 4–&, etc.

Sixteenth notes last for a quarter of a beat each, and you can fit 16 of them in a four-beat measure. A standard way to count sixteenth notes is: 1-e-&-a, 2-e-&-a, 3-e-&-a, 4-e-&-a, etc. Try playing the following on your bass while counting the syllables aloud.

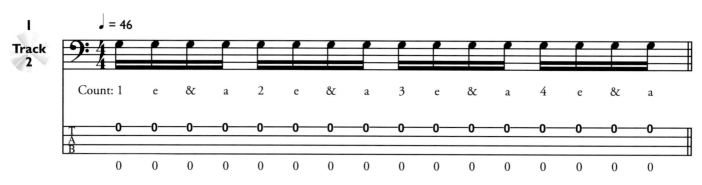

If you prefer, use the following syllables to count sixteenth notes: 1-six-teenth-note, 2-six-teenth-note, 3-six-teenth-note, 4-six-teenth-note, etc.

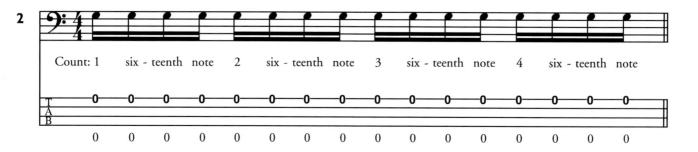

You can use either method above to count sixteenth notes; you could even come up with your own syllables. However, in this book, we will use the method demonstrated in Example 1.

Playing Sixteenth-Note Rhythms

To play sixteenth-note rhythms, it is best to alternate between the 1st (index) and 2nd (middle) fingers of your right hand. You should always strive for an even, consistent sound between the two fingers.

Following are some sixteenth-note exercises to get you counting and playing these rhythms correctly.

In the following example, you will be playing a different open string every four beats. Make sure you alternate the fingers of your right hand with each sixteenth note (right-hand fingering is indicated above the staff).

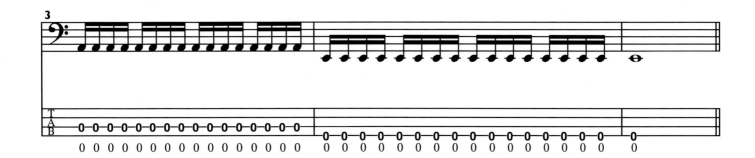

In the example below, you will be playing a different open string every two beats.

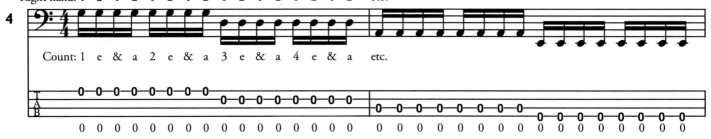

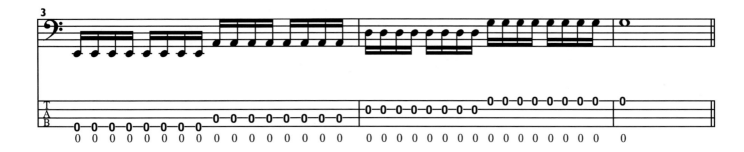

In the next exercise, you will play a different open string every beat. Before moving to each new open string, it is important to stop the previous string from ringing by *damping* it with a left-hand finger. This is done by lightly touching the string without pressing it against the fretboard. Remember to count the sixteenth notes as you did in the previous examples.

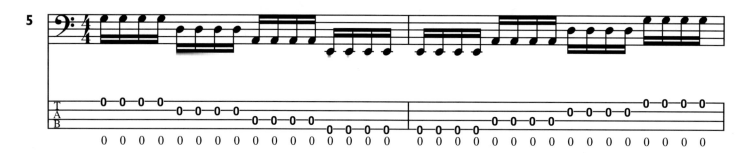

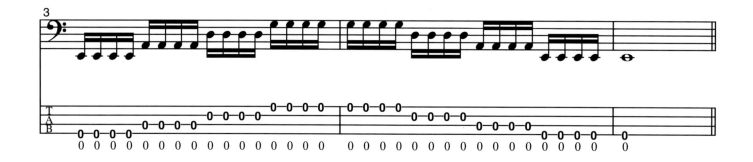

In the exercise below, you will be switching strings every half beat. It is important for your right-hand plucking to be as clean and precise as possible. Also, when switching to a new string, focus on damping each previous string to avoid any unwanted ringing. Good string damping is essential to funk bass. Mastering this technique now will help you better execute the bass lines that come later in the book.

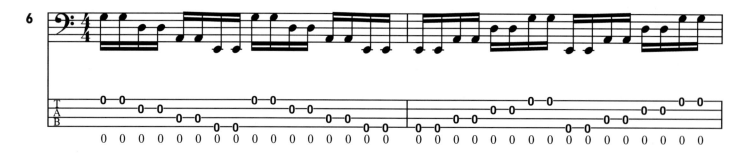

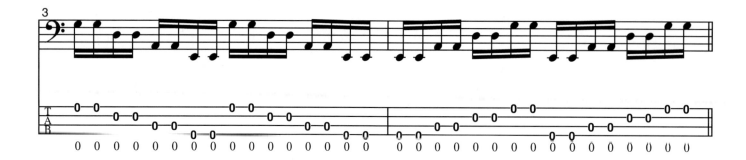

Syncopation

Syncopation occurs in a rhythm when the emphasis is shifted to a beat, or part of a beat, that is not normally emphasized. Syncopation is used in a variety of styles including ska, ragtime, jazz, and rock; it is also a major element of funk.

Missed-Beat Syncopation

In *missed-beat syncopation,* the absence of a note throws off the expected flow of the rhythm. In Example 7, a rest takes the place of an expected quarter note on beat 3, shifting the emphasis to beat 4. In even-numbered time signatures ($\frac{4}{4}$, $\frac{2}{4}$, etc.), the emphasis is usually placed on beats 1 and 3.

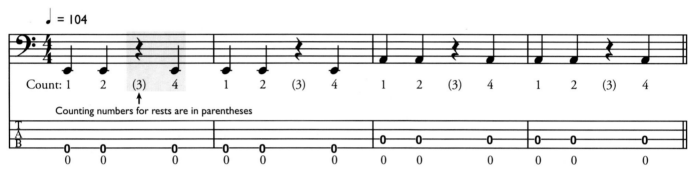

Extended-Note Syncopation

Extended-note syncopation can occur when note values are extended, through the use of ties, across measures. In the following example, the half notes and tied quarter notes create several points of syncopation. In each measure, emphasis is shifted from the third beat to the fourth beat. In measures 2 and 4, emphasis is shifted from the first beat to the second.

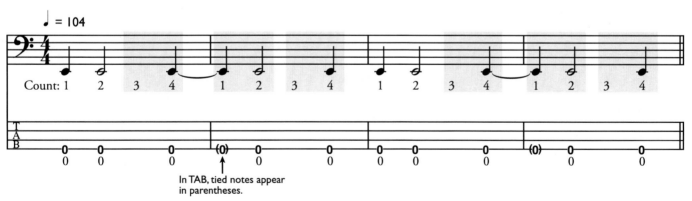

The examples above show that syncopation can occur even in uncomplicated rhythms made up of quarter notes and half notes. However, funk rhythms often consist of syncopated eighth- and sixteenth-note rhythms, so we'll start looking at some of these on the next page.

Offbeat Syncopation

When the emphasis of a beat is somewhere other than *on* the beat (1, 2, 3, or 4), this is known as *offbeat syncopation*. In eighth-note rhythms, offbeat syncopation occurs when emphasis is shifted to the "&s."

Below is an example of offbeat syncopation in which all of the "&s" are emphasized.

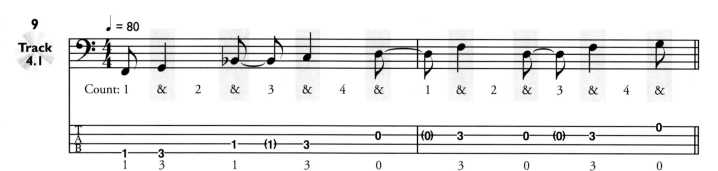

Creating Syncopation by Accenting Offbeats

The symbol > indicates an *accent*. When this sign is placed above or below a note, the note should be emphasized, or stressed.

Following is an eighth-note rhythm with accents placed on the beats.

> = Accent

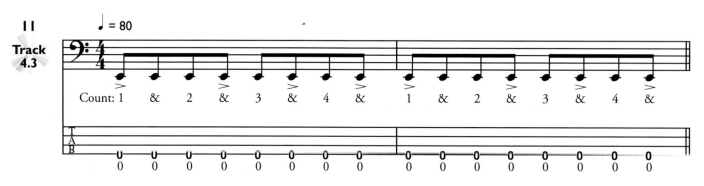

Now, let's take the rhythm from above and accent different parts of the measure. By placing the accents on the "&s" of beats 2, 3, and 4, we get a cool Latin-flavored rhythm.

Offbeat Syncopation with Sixteenth Notes

The most common rhythms used in funk bass lines are syncopated sixteenth-note rhythms. These can look difficult, so it is important to be able to subdivide the beats by counting 1-e-&-a, 2-e-&-a, etc. Play through them slowly at first, and strive for precision over speed!

In the rhythm below, extended notes are used to help shift the emphasis to the weak parts of the beats. This can be seen, for example, on the "e" and "a" of beat 2.

In the example below, eighth rests are used to shift the emphasis to the weak parts of the beats. Count this one carefully!

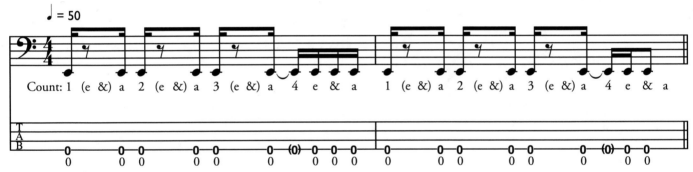

Below, eighth rests and sixteenth rests are used to shift the emphasis to the weak parts of the beats.

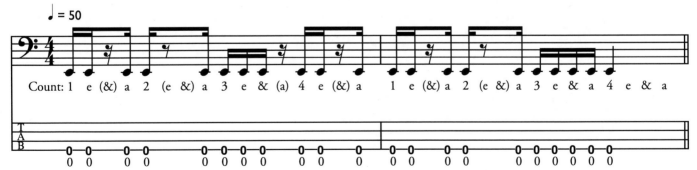

Muting

Muting is an essential funk bass technique, and it contributes to the funkiness of a bass line as much as the notes themselves. Muting is similar to damping (page 16), however, the objective here is to play the damped, or muted, note rather than just stop it from ringing.

Left-Hand Muting

Left-hand muting is the most common way to produce muted notes, and it is the technique used in this book. This is achieved by gently touching the fingers of the left hand on the string, without pressing it to the fretboard, and plucking the string with your right hand. The result is a percussive sound with no discernible pitch. Jaco Pastorius and Rocco Prestia are masters of this technique.

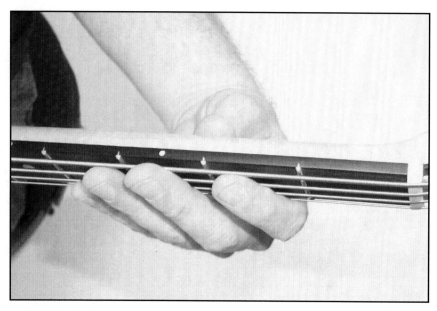

Left-hand muting.

Muted notes are indicated by an "X" notehead and are written on the line or space of the string to be played. For example, if you are playing a muted A string, an X notehead would appear in the standard notation on the space designating the A note. In TAB, an X appears on the string that is to be played.

15
Track 6

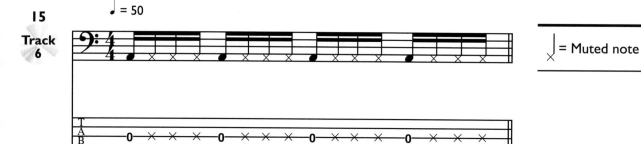

On the following page, we'll look at two more muting techniques. Although they are not specifically called for in this book, experiment with them once you have mastered the left-hand muting technique.

Palm Muting

Palm muting is a common guitar technique but it can also be used to play muted notes on the bass. Usually, this technique is used when plucking (not slapping) notes with the thumb. This is a classic funk playing style that, although not covered in this book, is fun to experiment with. A palm mute is achieved by resting the edge of your right-hand palm across the strings. Make sure enough of the palm is on the string to prevent any plucked string from vibrating. This technique may feel a bit awkward at first but the more you do it, the easier it will become.

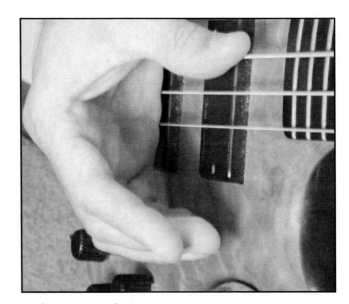

Palm muting technique.

3rd-and-4th-Finger Muting

The *3rd-and-4th-finger muting* technique is used in fingerstyle funk only. This technique is achieved by placing the 3rd and 4th fingers of your right hand on the string you will be plucking. Make sure you are touching the string enough to prevent any vibrations from occurring. Players will often pluck the strings with the thumb while using this muting technique.

3rd-and-4th-finger muting technique.

Muted notes will appear in many examples in this book. As mentioned on the previous page, use the left-hand muting technique when muted notes are indicated. Once you have mastered left-hand muting, experiment with the techniques on this page. You may find that one of these works better for certain bass lines.

Syncopated Eighth-Note Rhythms
Using Muted Notes

The following examples feature syncopated eighth-note rhythms with muted notes. What makes them syncopated is the placement of the unmuted notes. You may experiment with the three techniques discussed on the previous pages, but the left-hand muting technique will probably work the best.

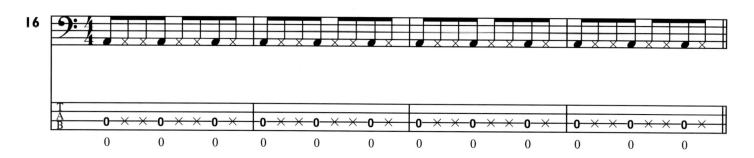

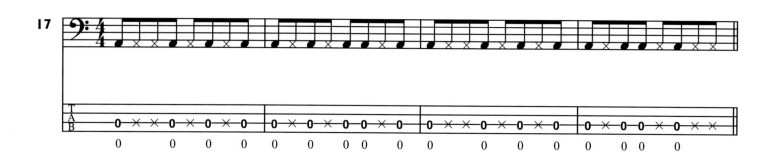

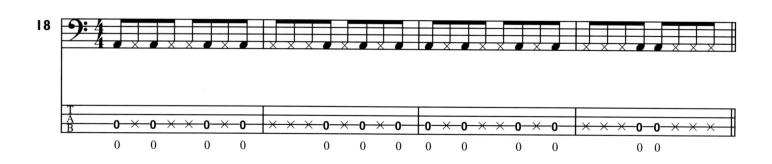

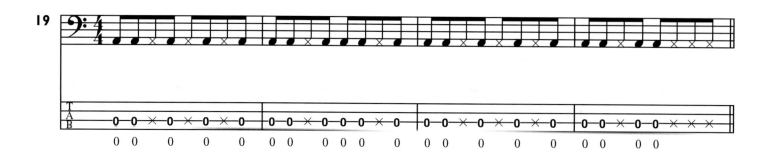

Syncopated Sixteenth-Note Rhythms
Using Muted Notes

The examples below feature syncopated sixteenth-note rhythms with muted notes. These will help you prepare for the bass lines that come later in the book. Remember to practice these examples slowly at first and to count carefully. Also, make sure to alternate the 1st and 2nd fingers of your right hand when plucking, and mute the strings with the fingers of your left-hand when playing muted notes.

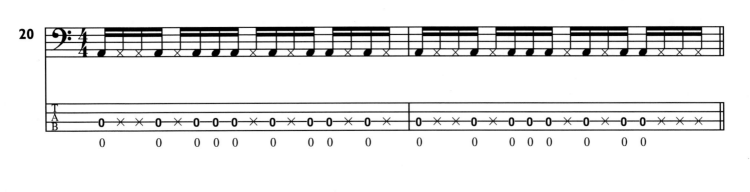

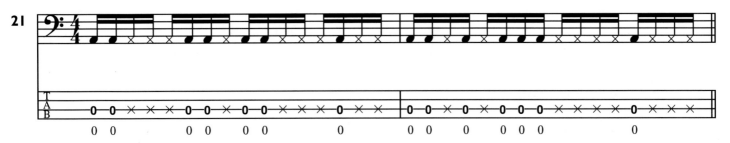

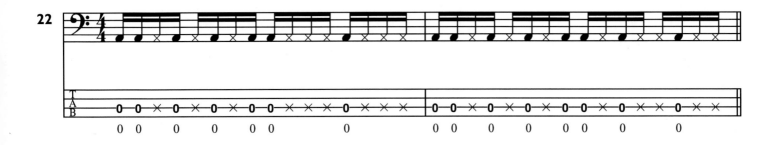

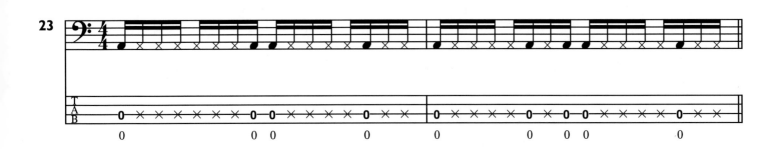

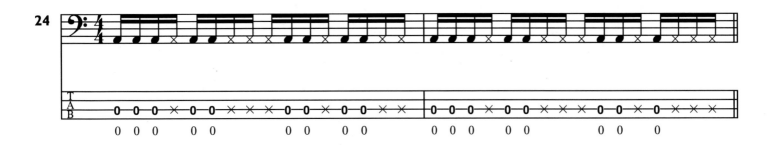

More Syncopation

As we've said, syncopation is one of the main characteristics of funk bass. Tapping, clapping, or singing syncopated rhythms is an excellent way to prepare for the funk bass lines you will encounter in this book.

In this section, we'll be playing rhythms that are close to actual bass lines. At first, practice clapping, tapping, or singing these rhythms until you are comfortable; then, play them on your bass. At this point, it is not important what notes you use to play the rhythms; mastering the rhythms themselves will make it easier for you later when different pitches are added.

When practicing the following examples, start at a slow tempo and count carefully. It is best to practice with a metronome, drum machine, or computer software such as GarageBand. Choose a tempo that you are comfortable with, then gradually increase the speed. If you were to do this for 5 to 10 minutes, you would be amazed at the progress you could make. (Note: It is recommended that you use this practice method for *all* of the examples in this book.)

Syncopated Rhythms Using Quarter Notes, Eighth Notes, and Rests

We'll start with quarter- and eighth-note rhythms. Remember to divide the beat when counting eighth notes (1-&, 2-&, 3-&, 4-&, etc.).

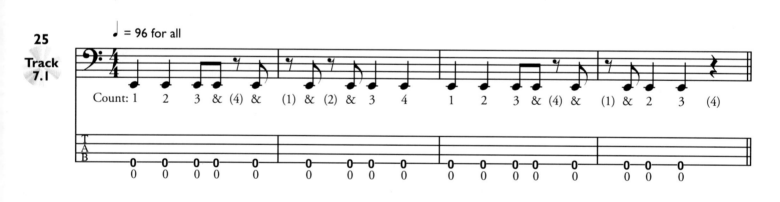

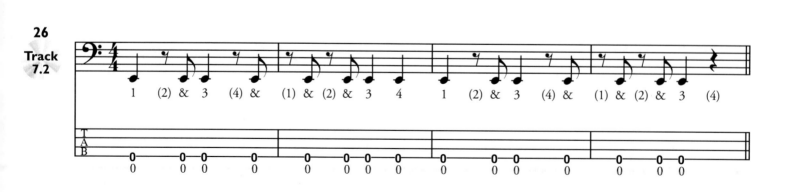

27

Track 7.3

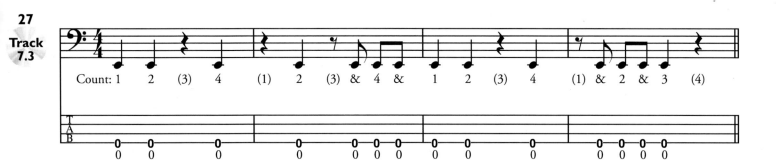

Count: 1   2   (3)   4   (1)   2   (3)   &   4   &   1   2   (3)   4   (1)   &   2   &   3   (4)

28

Track 7.4

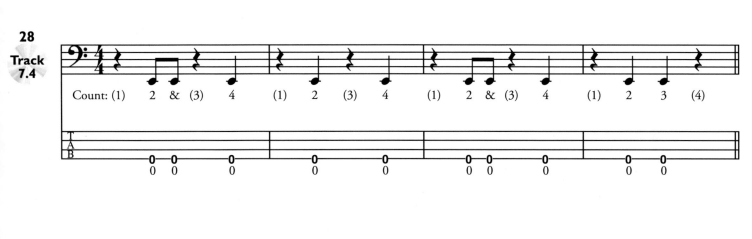

Count: (1)   2   &   (3)   4   (1)   2   (3)   4   (1)   2   &   (3)   4   (1)   2   3   (4)

29

Track 7.5

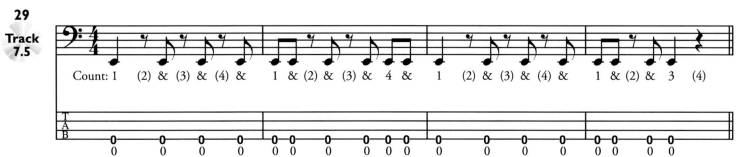

Count: 1   (2)   &   (3)   &   (4)   &   1   &   (2)   &   (3)   &   4   &   1   (2)   &   (3)   &   (4)   &   1   &   (2)   &   3   (4)

30

Track 7.6

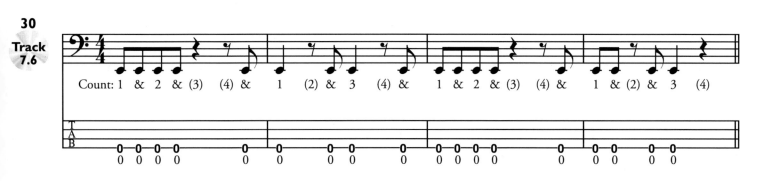

Count: 1   &   2   &   (3)   (4)   &   1   (2)   &   3   (4)   &   1   &   2   &   (3)   (4)   &   1   &   (2)   &   3   (4)

31

Track 7.7

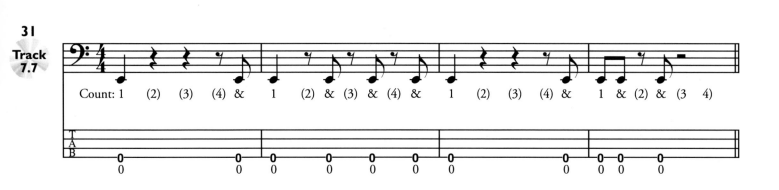

Count: 1   (2)   (3)   (4)   &   1   (2)   &   (3)   &   (4)   &   1   (2)   (3)   (4)   &   1   &   (2)   &   (3   4)

Syncopated Rhythms Using Eighth Notes, Sixteenth Notes, and Rests

The following rhythms include sixteenth notes and rests. Remember to count them as 1-e-&-a, 2-e-&-a, etc. Like the examples on the previous pages, practice clapping, tapping, or singing these rhythms slowly at first, then gradually increase the tempos. When you are comfortable, try to play them on your bass.

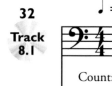
32
Track 8.1

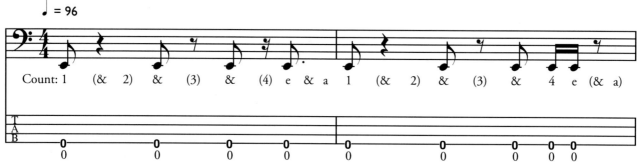

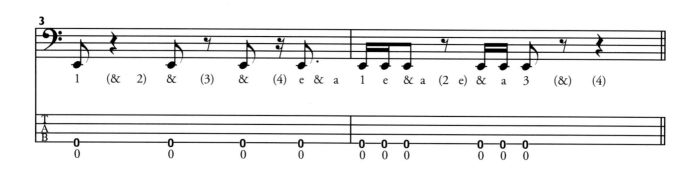

33
Track 8.2

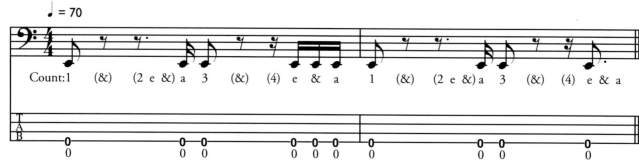

34
Track 8.3

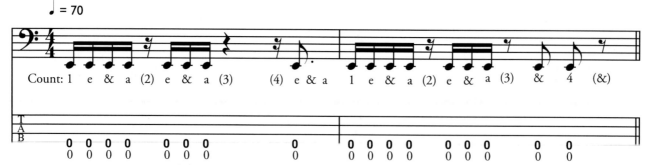

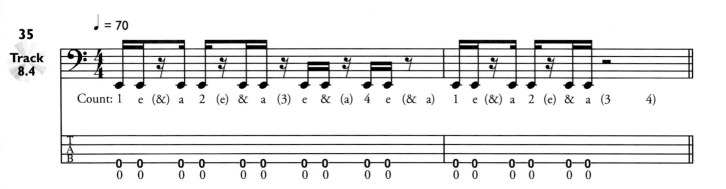

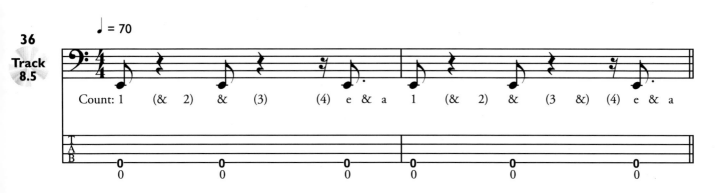

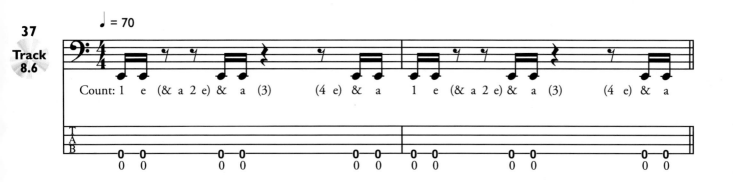

A Note About Articulation

When playing any instrument, it's important to remember that it is not *how many* notes you play (and, often, not even *what* notes you play), but *how you play them*. How loudly or softly do you play a note? Do you accent a particular note or play it quieter than other notes in the group? Do you play the bass line with a *staccato* feel (short, detached) or with a *legato* feel (smooth and flowing). Will you mute notes or leave them unmuted? These are all questions regarding *articulation*—how particular phrases are expressed, or played. It's very important not just to play the notes on the paper, but to breathe life into them by playing with expression, passion, and emotion, so that

when combined with good technique, you are creating great music. The way you articulate helps define who you are as a player and separates you from any other bassist. We could all play a four-bar groove with the same notes, but the *way* we play it is what makes each of us different. The main goal is to develop your own sound and be unique in your own way.

In the next couple of chapters, we will look "behind the scenes" at concepts that will help you better understand funk bass and music in general.

Chapter 3: Scales, Intervals, and Modes

The Major Scale

A *scale* is a series of notes in a particular pattern. Perhaps the most important scale for a bassist to learn is the *major scale*. By understanding the major scale, you can understand many other musical concepts, including modes, chord construction, chord progressions, and soloing.

The major scale has seven notes, and each note can be referred to by its *scale degree* (1–2–3–4–5–6–7). Notice in the scale below there is an 8th degree; this is the *octave* of the 1st scale degree. An octave is the distance of 12 half

steps between two notes with the same name. The first scale degree is also called the *tonic*.

Below is a C Major scale. Notice the sequence of whole steps (W) and half steps (H). This formula (W–W–H–W–W–W–H) is the same for every major scale.

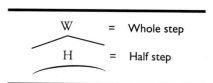

C Major Scale

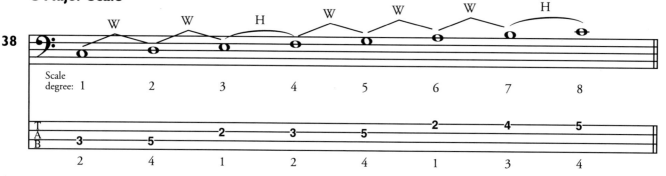

The fingering indicated above shows the most common way to play this scale. The 24-124-134 fingering allows you to play the scale in one position without having to move up or down the fretboard.

Knowing the major scale's sequence of whole steps and half steps makes it easy to create a different major scale starting on any note. If you play the G note on the 3rd fret of the 4th string and follow the same pattern of whole steps and half steps shown above, the result is a G Major scale.

G Major Scale

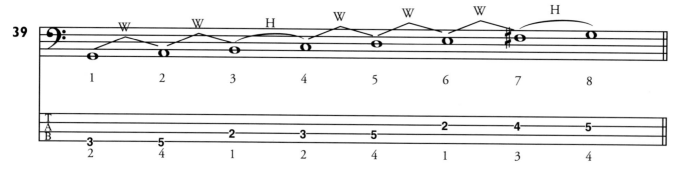

Keys and Key Signatures

When a song or piece of music is based on a particular scale, it is said to be in the *key* of that scale. For example, if a song is based on the G Major scale, it is in the key of G Major, or the key of G.

A *key signature* is a group of sharps or flats at the beginning of a staff that indicate the key. For example, in the key of G, there is one sharp, F♯. In other words, all F notes will be sharped unless otherwise indicated. The key signature for G Major looks like this:

Major Scale Fingerings

In addition to the fingering shown on the previous page, there are many possible fingerings for the major scale. The more ways you learn to play the scale, the better off you'll be when applying it to real music.

Following are three common ways to play a *one-octave* major scale. By "one-octave," we mean from the tonic to the octave above the tonic. All of the scale and arpeggio fingerings in this book are *moveable,* meaning you can start them from any location on the fretboard. For example, if you start Fingering 1 below from the G on the 3rd fret of the 4th string, you would get a G Major scale. If you start from the A on the 5th fret of the 4th string, you would get an A Major scale.

One-Octave Major Scale Fingerings

Fingering 1

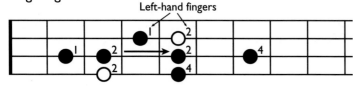

○ = Tonic.

⟶ = *Position shift.* Move your left hand to a new position on the fretboard.

Fingering 2

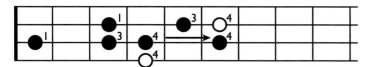

Fingering 3

Now, we'll look at a couple of *two-octave* major scale fingerings. By two-octave, we mean from the tonic to two octaves above the tonic.

Two-Octave Major Scale Fingerings

Fingering 1

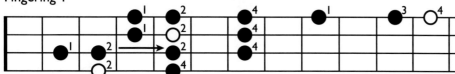

Fingering 2

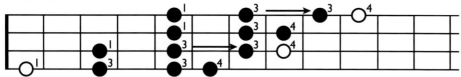

Intervals

An *interval* is the distance between two notes. Understanding intervals is important to musicians, as we often need to think about relationships between notes when creating chords and scales.

All of the intervals found in the major scale are *major* or *perfect* intervals. If you make a major interval smaller by one half step, it becomes *minor*. If you make a perfect interval smaller by one half step, it becomes *diminished*. If you make a perfect or major interval larger by a half step, it becomes *augmented*. Below are the intervals within one octave above the note C.

The Intervals

Perfect unison (P.U.)	Minor 2nd (m2)	Major 2nd (M2)	Minor 3rd (m3)	Major 3rd (M3)

Perfect 4th (P4)	Augmented 4th (A4)	Diminished 5th (d5)	Perfect 5th (P5)	Augmented 5th (A5)

Minor 6th (m6)	Major 6th (M6)	Minor 7th (m7)	Major 7th (M7)	Perfect octave (P.O.)

Jaco Pastorius hit the scene in 1976. In that single year, he recorded with Pat Metheny, Weather Report, and Al DiMeola, and recorded his own self-titled debut album. Since then, Jaco has influenced countless musicians and is considered one of the greatest bassists of all time.

Modes of the Major Scale

A *mode* is a "reordering" of notes from a scale. Each tone of the major scale is the starting note for a different mode. There are seven tones in the major scale so there are seven modes. When you play any major scale starting and ending on the tonic, you can think of it as the first mode of the scale. When you play any major scale starting and ending on the 2nd degree, you can think of it as the second mode of that scale, and so on. The modes of the major scale are: *Ionian* (also known as the major scale), *Dorian, Phrygian, Lydian, Mixolydian, Aeolian* (also known as the *natural minor scale,* see page 37), and *Locrian.*

Relative Thinking

Shown below are the seven modes of the C Major scale. Each mode is created by starting and ending on a different note of the C Major scale. This is called *relative thinking* because we are relating each note to the C Major scale.

Notice in each mode there are two half steps that occur between different scale degrees. For example, in the Ionian mode, the half steps occur between the 3rd and 4th tones and the 7th and 8th tones. In the Dorian mode, the half steps occur between the 2nd and 3rd tones and the 6th and 7th tones. It is the order of the whole steps and half steps that gives each mode its distinct and unique sound. In the modes below, the half steps are highlighted. (Fingerings for the modes are on pages 33–36.)

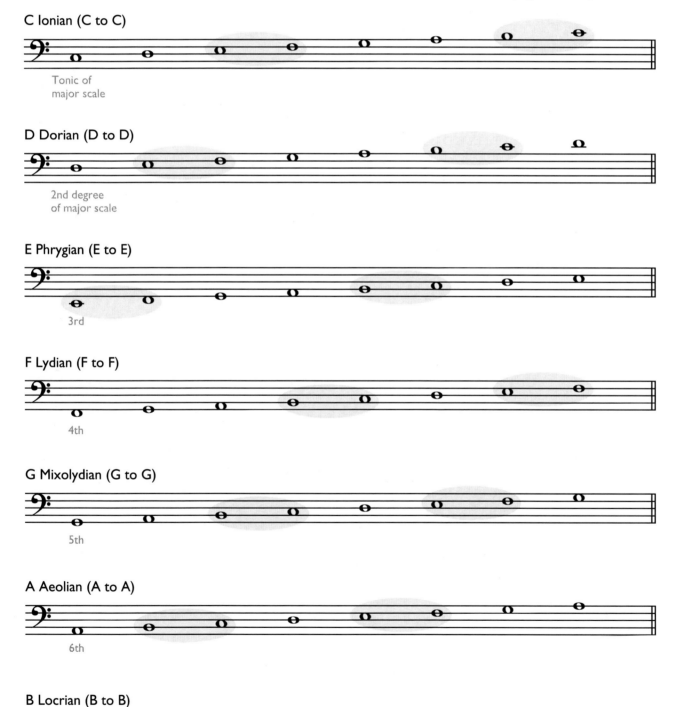

C Ionian (C to C)

Tonic of major scale

D Dorian (D to D)

2nd degree of major scale

E Phrygian (E to E)

3rd

F Lydian (F to F)

4th

G Mixolydian (G to G)

5th

A Aeolian (A to A)

6th

B Locrian (B to B)

7th

Parallel Thinking

If we were to play each of the modes starting and ending on the same root, we would be playing *parallel* modes; this is known as *parallel thinking*. Each mode is created with the same order of whole steps and half steps shown on the previous page, but we are now building each mode starting on the tonic C.

When discussing parallel modes we compare each note to a major scale with the same root. For example, if we are in C and the 7th is B♭, we think of the B♭ as a ♭7 because it has been lowered from its position in a C Major scale. This way of thinking is helpful for learning which notes

are unique to each mode. (This system is also useful for learning other chords and scale types as well.)

Below are the seven modes built on the note C. The whole steps and half steps for each mode are the same as on the previous page. The tones that are characteristic to each mode are shown. For example, the C Dorian mode has a ♭3 (E♭) and a ♭7 (B♭). These two scale degrees are characteristic of the Dorian mode when compared to a major scale of the same root.

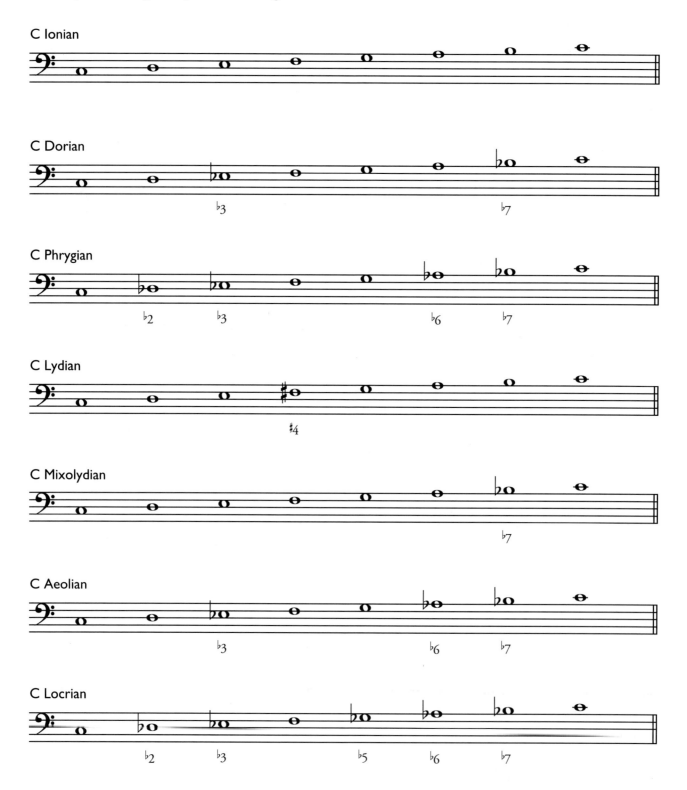

Fingerings for Major Scale Modes

Since the modes are an important part of your musical vocabulary, memorizing fingerings for each of them is beneficial to your playing. In funk music, the Dorian and Mixolydian modes are more important than the others. The chord type most commonly used in funk is the dominant 7th chord. The "chord scale" used to play bass lines over the dominant 7th chord is the Mixolydian mode, therefore it is the most useful mode to funk bass players. (A "chord scale" is simply a scale that corresponds to a particular chord.)

The next most common chord in funk music is the minor, or minor 7th, chord. The mode used to play over minor and minor 7th chords is usually the Dorian mode. Since Mixolydian and Dorian are the two most commonly used modes in funk, pay particular attention to them when learning the following fingerings. Remember that all of these fingerings are moveable.

C Ionian

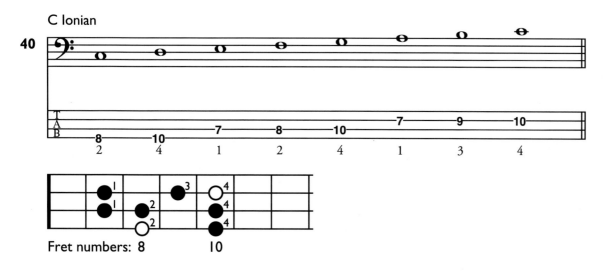

C Dorian

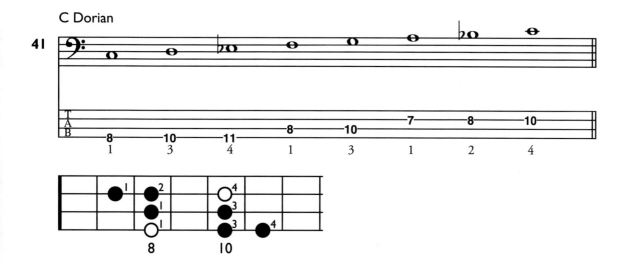

C Phrygian

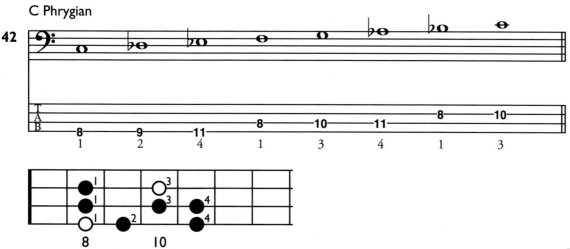

C Lydian

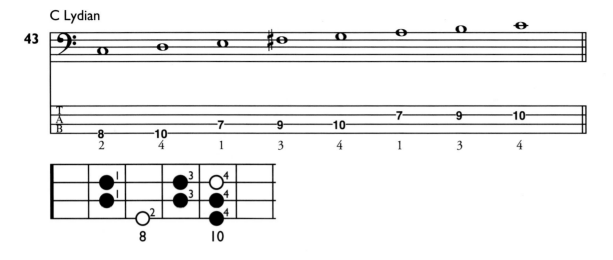

C Mixolydian

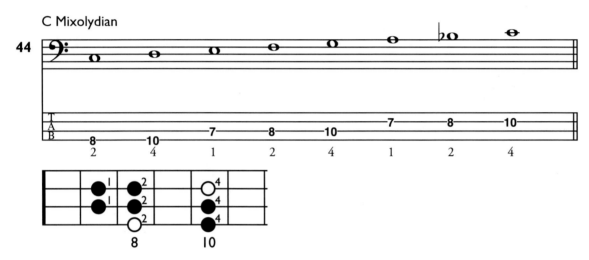

C Aeolian

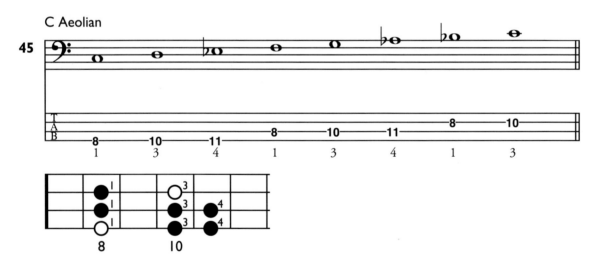

C Locrian

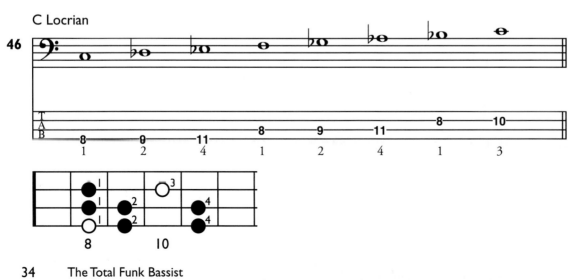

Additional Mixolydian and Dorian Fingerings

As noted on page 33, the most commonly used modes in funk bass are the Mixolydian and Dorian modes. In this book, you will find many funk bass lines derived from these two modes. The more you listen to and learn funk bass lines, the more you will realize the significant role they play.

The previous pages showed one-octave fingerings for the modes. Since you will use the Mixolydian and Dorian modes most often, let's examine more fingering possibilities for each.

One-Octave Mixolydian Mode Fingerings

Fingering 1

Fingering 2

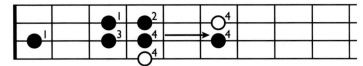

Two-Octave Mixolydian Mode Fingerings

Fingering 1

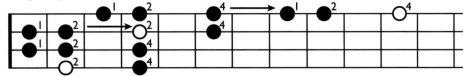

Fingering 2

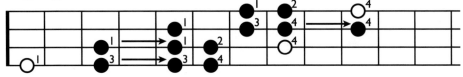

One-Octave Dorian Mode Fingerings

Fingering 1

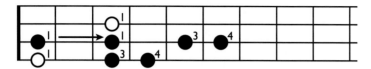

Fingering 2

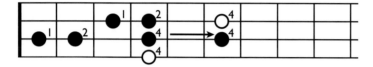

Two-Octave Dorian Mode Fingerings

Fingering 1

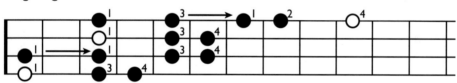

Fingering 2

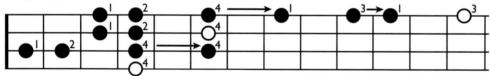

The Natural Minor Scale

For every major scale, there is a *natural minor scale* with the same key signature. This is called the *relative minor scale*. If we apply relative thinking (page 31) to the modes, then the A Natural Minor scale is the same as the C Major scale starting and ending on the 6th degree. In fact, if you start and end on the 6th degree of any major scale, you will be playing its relative minor scale. If you remember the modes, the Aeolian mode starts and ends on the 6th degree of the major scale, thus, the natural minor scale is another name for the Aeolian mode.

C Major Scale (Two Octaves)

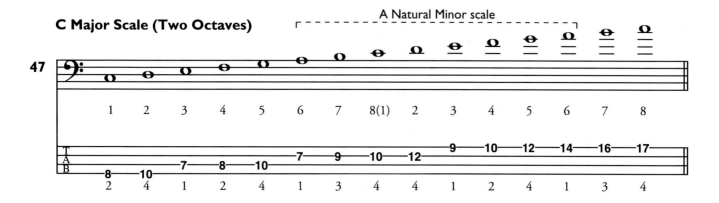

The sequence of whole steps and half steps that creates a natural minor scale is different from that of a major scale (see below).

```
W  H  W  W  H  W  W
∧  ∩  ∧  ∧  ∩  ∧  ∧
A  B  C  D  E  F  G  A
```

When we compare the A Natural Minor to the A Major scale (see Parallel Thinking, page 32), the 3rd, 6th and 7th degrees are lowered and therefore referred to as the *minor* scale degrees. The minor scale degrees are indicated with a flat sign: ♭3, ♭6 and ♭7. These minor notes are the characteristic notes of the natural minor scale.

Since they are essentially the same scale, fingerings for the natural minor scale will be the same as for the Aeolian mode.

A Natural Minor Scale

The Harmonic Minor Scale

The *harmonic minor* scale is similar to the natural minor scale except it has a natural 7th. The harmonic minor scale is darker and more exotic sounding than the natural minor scale.

A Harmonic Minor Scale

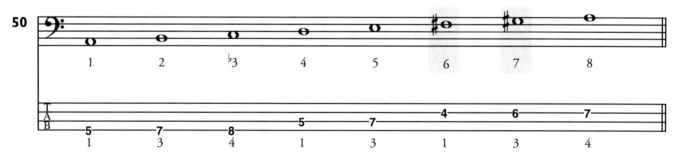

The Melodic Minor Scale

The *melodic minor* scale, also known as the *jazz minor* scale, is like the natural minor scale but with a natural 6th and 7th. You can also think of the melodic minor scale as a major scale with a ♭3. The only difference between an A Major scale and an A Melodic Minor scale is that the A Melodic Minor scale has a C, or ♭3. Because of this ♭3, or minor 3rd, the melodic minor scale has a darker sound than the major scale.

A Melodic Minor Scale

The modes of the harmonic and melodic minor scales sound more exotic than those of the major scale, and they have many uses as well. For instance, the modes of the melodic minor scale are commonly used by jazz musicians for improvisation and harmony.

To learn about the modes of these minor scales, refer to *The Total Jazz Bassist* (Alfred #26064).

The Major Pentatonic Scale

A *pentatonic scale* is a five-note scale. The most common types of pentatonic scales are the *major pentatonic* and the *minor pentatonic* scales. Both the major and minor pentatonic scales are used often in funk, rock, blues, and jazz.

The major pentatonic scale is used to create bass lines over major chords. It consists of scale degrees 1, 2, 3, 5, and 6 of the major scale. Basically, the major pentatonic is the major scale without the 4th and 7th scale degrees.

C Major Pentatonic Scale

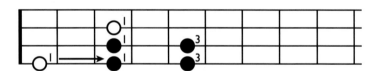

Major Pentatonic Fingerings

Below are a couple of additional fingerings for the major pentatonic scale. Get comfortable with both the one- and two-octave fingerings. Then, try to come up with some of your own.

One-Octave Fingering

Two-Octave Fingering

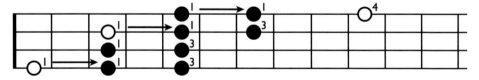

The Minor Pentatonic Scale

The minor pentatonic scale is often used for improvising in funk, rock, blues, and jazz. It consists of scale degrees 1, ♭3, 4, 5, and ♭7.

C Minor Pentatonic Scale

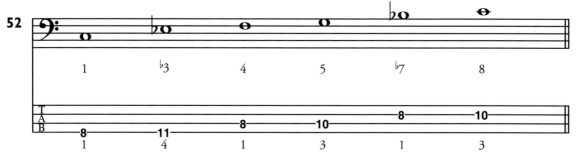

The minor pentatonic scale can be used to create bass lines over minor chords, minor 7th chords, and even "5" chords. The 5 chord, also known as the *power chord*, consists of a *root* and 5th, the root being the note upon which the chord is built and from which it gets its name. For example, if our root was E and we added a B, which is a 5th above it, we would have an E5 chord.

Although the minor pentatonic scale is not used for bass lines over major chords or dominant chords, it can be used for soloing over a wide variety of chords and chord progressions.

Minor Pentatonic Fingerings

Following are a couple of additional fingerings for the minor pentatonic scale. Get them under your fingers, then try to come up with your own.

One-Octave Fingering

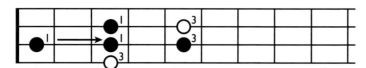

Two-Octave Fingering

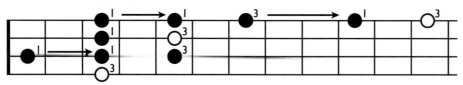

The Blues Scale

The *blues scale* is perhaps the most widely used scale by beginning funk, jazz, and blues improvisers and is a stepping-stone to more sophisticated sounding scales. It is similar to a minor pentatonic scale but with an added ♭5. The blues scale consists of the tones 1, ♭3, 4, ♭5, 5, and ♭7. The ♭3, ♭5, and ♭7 are known as *blue notes* and are essential to the sound of the blues and all blues-based music like funk and rock.

C Blues Scale

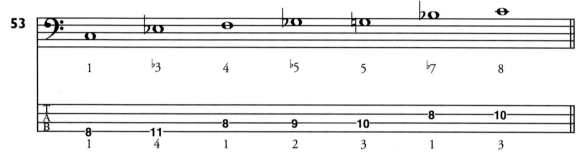

The blues scale is often used for improvisation in a variety of styles, and it is also used to create bass lines over minor chords, 5 chords, and in riff-oriented tunes. Like the major and minor pentatonic, the blues scale is a useful scale to get under your fingers.

Blues Scale Fingerings

Following are a couple of additional fingerings for the blues scale. After you feel comfortable with these, see if you can figure out some fingerings of your own.

One-Octave Fingering

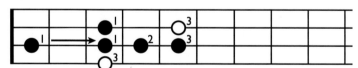

Two-Octave Fingering

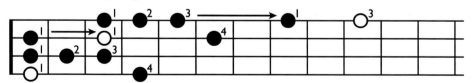

Chapter 4: Chords

Triads

A chord is two or more notes played simultaneously to create *harmony.* The responsibility of a bassist (in addition to laying down the groove) is to outline the harmony, or chord progression, of the tune. To outline the harmony, bassists often play arpeggios, which are the notes of chords played separately rather than simultaneously.

A *triad* is a three-note chord. Triads are the building blocks of harmony, so it's important to become familiar with them. There are four types of triads: *major, minor, diminished,* and *augmented.* Major triads consist of a root, 3rd, and 5th. Minor triads consist of a root, ♭3rd, and 5th. Diminished triads have a root, ♭3rd, and ♭5th. Augmented triads have a root, 3rd, and ♯5th. In funk music, the major and minor triads are found more commonly than the diminished and augmented triads.

Following are fingerings for the four types of triads.

Major

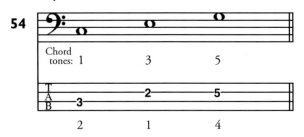 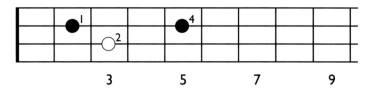

Minor

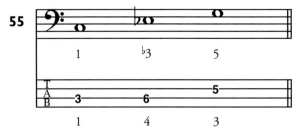 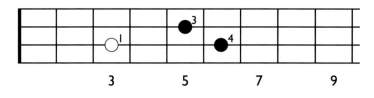

Diminished

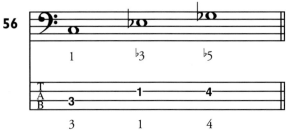 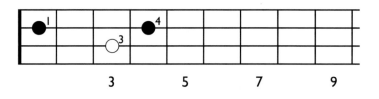

Augmented

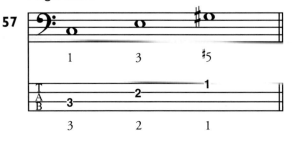 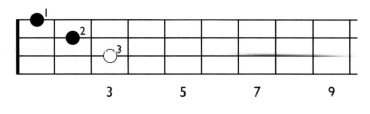

7th Chords

Now, let's look at *7th chords*. A 7th chord is a four-note chord. Though many types of 7th chords are used in jazz and pop, those most often used in funk are the *dominant 7th* and *minor 7th*. However, it is a good idea to get all of the chord types under your fingers because it can make you a more interesting and well-rounded musician.

There are six types of 7th chords you should know: *major 7th*, dominant 7th, minor 7th, *minor 7♭5*, diminished 7th, and *minor major 7th*. Following are fingerings for these types of 7th chords.

Major 7th

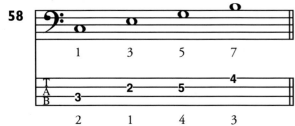 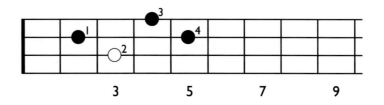

Dominant 7th

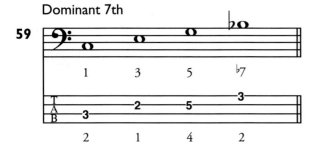 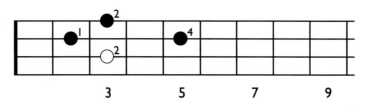

Minor 7th

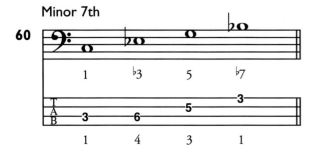 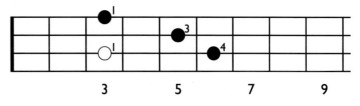

Minor 7♭5

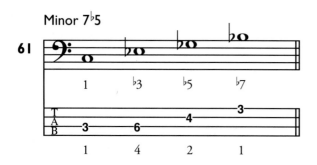
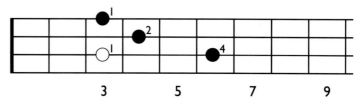

Diminished 7th

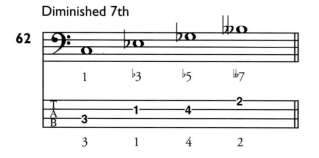
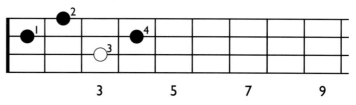

Minor Major 7th

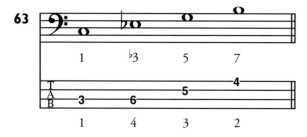
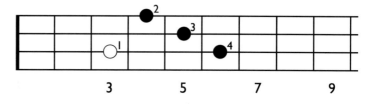

Again, pay particular attention to the dominant 7th and minor 7th arpeggios, as they are the most popular 7th chords in funk.

One-chord funk jams usually consist of one dominant 7th chord (a funk in "E" is on an E7). Two-chord funk tunes often consist of a minor 7th and a dominant 7th (for example, Amin7 to D7).

Chord Symbols

The chart below shows the most commonly used chord symbols. There is no standardization of chord symbols, meaning some composers may use some over others. For this reason, it's a good idea to become familiar with all of the symbols that are used to indicate particular chord types. For each chord type, the notes that make up that chord have been listed (for example: 1–3–5 for a major chord.

CHORD SYMBOL CHART

				Used in this book
Major 1–3–5	C	C△	CMaj	C
Minor 1–♭3–5	Cmin	Cm	C–	Cmin
Diminished 1–♭3–♭5	C°	Cdim		Cdim
Augmented 1–3–♯5	C+	Caug	CMaj♯5	Caug
Major 6th 1–3–5–6	C6	C△6	CMaj6	C6
Major 7th 1–3–5–7	CMaj7	C△7	CM7	CMaj7
Dominant 7th 1–3–5–♭7	C7	Cdom7		C7
Minor 7th 1–♭3–5–♭7	Cmin7	Cm7	C–7	Cmin7
Minor 7♭5 (Half Diminished) 1–♭3–♭5–♭7	C–7♭5	Cø7		Cmin7♭5
Diminished 7th 1–♭3–♭5–♭♭7 (6)	C°7	Cdim7		Cdim7
Minor Major 7th 1–♭3–5–7	Cmin(Maj7)	C–(△7)	Cmin(△7)	CminMaj7

Major Scale Diatonic Harmony

Many of the songs you listen to use the same chord progressions in different combinations. The study of major scale *diatonic harmony* will help you identify and become familiar with many of the most common chord progressions. *Diatonic* means "within the scale or key." "Harmony" (as we learned on page 42) refers to chords or chord progressions. The term "diatonic harmony" refers to chords built from a particular scale.

Because we want to get a firm understanding of the diatonic harmony of a major scale, we will explore the harmony built first in triads, then 7th chords.

Diatonic Triads

Each major key has its own specific set of triads. The way to create these triads is to "stack" diatonic thirds on each note of the scale. We will stack two consecutive 3rds on each note. Each triad is assigned a Roman numeral according to the scale degree on which it is built. For example, the chord built on the 4th degree of the scale is called the *four chord* and is indicated by the Roman numeral IV.

Each triad consists of two stacked 3rds. These 3rds can be either major or minor, depending on the scale degree. The result will be a major triad, a minor triad, or a diminished triad. Notice that uppercase Roman numerals are used for major triads, and lowercase Roman numerals are used for minor triads. A small circle next to a lowercase Roman numeral indicates a diminished triad; for example, vii°.

Diatonic Triads in the Key of C

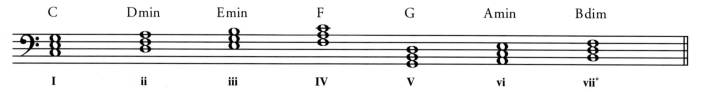

The sequence of chords in major scale diatonic harmony is the same in every key:

> I, IV, and V are major.
> ii, iii, and vi are minor.
> vii is diminished.

For example, check out the diatonic triads in the key of G (below). Notice the chord sequence is the same as in the key of C. The qualities of the chords remain the same, but the letter names change. For example, the IV chord in the key of C is F Major. In the key of G, the IV chord is still major in quality, but it is C Major.

Roman Numeral Review

I or i 1	V or v 5
II or ii 2	VI or vi 6
III or iii 3	VII or vii 7
IV or iv 4	

Diatonic Triads in the Key of G

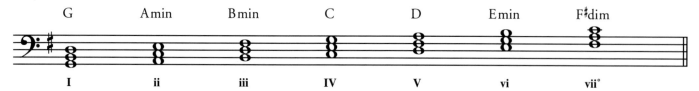

Diatonic 7th Chords

As with the diatonic triads, we stack consecutive 3rds on each note of the scale to create diatonic 7th chords. We stacked two consecutive 3rds to create triads; now, we must stack *three* consecutive 3rds to create 7th chords.

When we build the chords by stacking three consecutive 3rds, some of the chords will be major 7th, some will be minor 7th, one will be dominant 7th, and one will be minor 7♭5 (half-diminished). A lowercase Roman numeral followed by a small circle with a diagonal slash indicates a half-diminished 7th chord; for example, vii⌀.

Diatonic 7th Chords in the Key of C Major

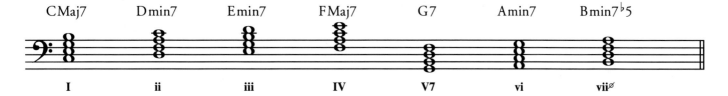

As with diatonic triads, the sequence of diatonic 7th chords is the same in every major key:

> I and IV are major 7th.
> ii, iii, and vi are minor 7th.
> V is dominant 7th.
> vii is minor 7♭5 (half diminished).

Below are the diatonic 7th chords in the key of G. Notice the chord sequence is the same as in the key of C; only the letter names are different.

Diatonic 7th Chords in the Key of G

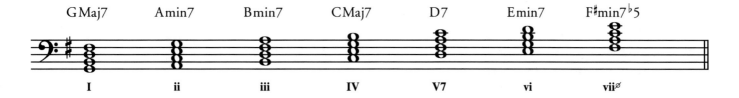

Minor Scale Diatonic Harmony

Remember, there are three forms of the minor scale: natural minor, harmonic minor, and melodic minor (see pages 37–38). Each scale has its own diatonic harmony. We'll skip discussing triads and jump straight to 7th chords because 7th chords are more commonly used in funk. (You can convert any 7th chord to a triad simply by omitting the 7th.)

Natural Minor Diatonic Harmony

Since the natural minor scale is built from the 6th degree of the major scale, it has the same chords, just in a different order. The C Natural Minor scale is the relative minor of E♭ Major, so it has the same exact chords as the E♭ Major scale. The Roman numerals are different because the vi chord in E♭ Major is the i chord in C Minor.

Diatonic 7th Chords for C Natural Minor

Harmonic Minor Diatonic Harmony

Because of the natural 7th scale degree, the harmonic minor scale has some unique chords. The i, iii, V, and vii chords include the major 7th scale degree, in this case the B♮, and therefore will be different in quality from the i, iii, V and vii chords of the natural minor. The V chord of the harmonic minor is significant because it is a dominant chord. The tension created by a dominant V chord is crucial in many types of music because it "wants" to resolve back to the home chord, or i chord. All major keys have a dominant V chord, as do the keys based on harmonic and melodic minor scales.

Diatonic 7th Chords for C Harmonic Minor

Melodic Minor Diatonic Harmony

Below are the chords derived from the melodic minor scale. Because of the natural 6th and 7th scale degrees, there are some unique chords here as well, including a dominant IV as well as a dominant V chord.

Diatonic 7th Chords for C Melodic Minor

Chapter 5: Starter Fingerstyle Funk Grooves

Now, it's time to have fun playing fingerstyle funk bass grooves. In fingerstyle funk, only the fingers are used to pluck the strings, and there is no slapping or popping. Some of the greatest bass lines in this style can be heard on any recording by James Jamerson, Jaco Pastorius, or Rocco Prestia. Listen to as much of their playing as possible to get the sound of this technique in your ears. Listening is a crucial aspect of learning to play music.

In this chapter, you'll be playing starter funk bass grooves. They're called "starter" grooves because they start out simple and gradually become more challenging. We'll begin by using just the root of the chord, then add the octave, the 5th, the 3rd, and the 7th.

Remember that funk music is more about the rhythm than harmonic or melodic content (though these are important too), so focus on playing the rhythms precisely by using a metronome.

Using the Root

Fairly simple funk bass lines can also sound great and be very effective; the rhythm is what makes them funky. The following funk bass grooves are made using only the root of the chord. Pay close attention to the muted notes, and most of all, have fun!

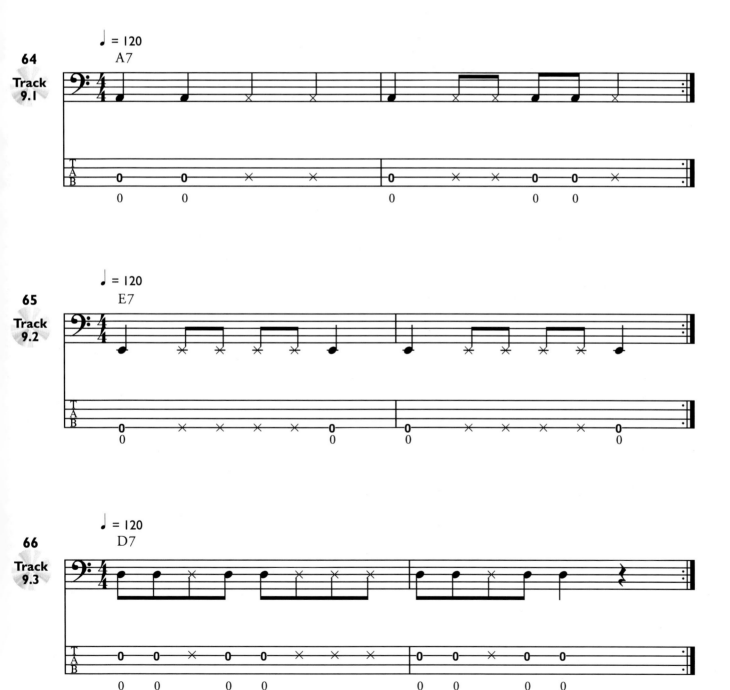

Note the use of sixteenth notes in the following bass grooves. Even though only the roots are being used, the rhythms are starting to get good and funky. Count carefully and be rhythmically precise when playing the following examples.

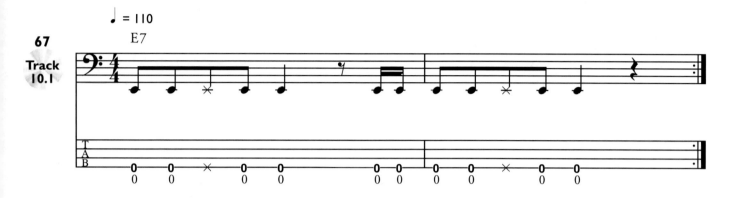

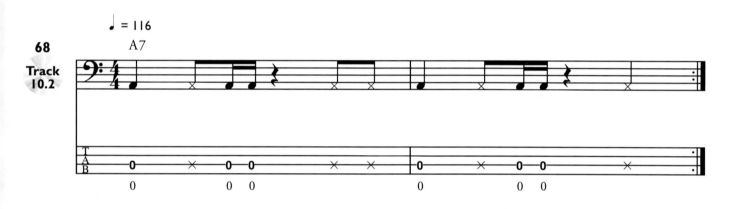

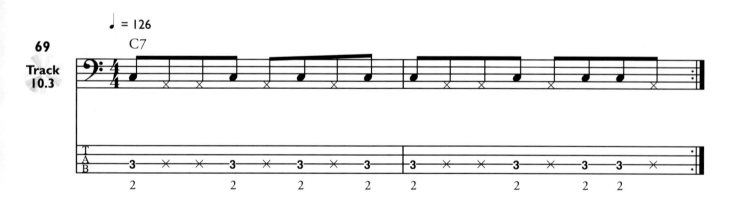

In the tune below, the bass line uses only the roots of the chords being played. This is a great example of how a funk bass line can be harmonically simple but still *groove*.

On the CD, the bass is panned to the left. If you turn your stereo's balance control to the right, you can eliminate the bass part and play along with the backing track.

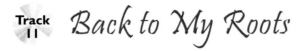

Track 11 *Back to My Roots*

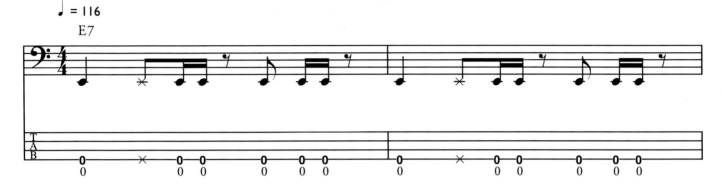

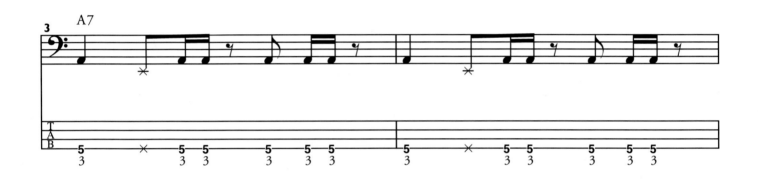

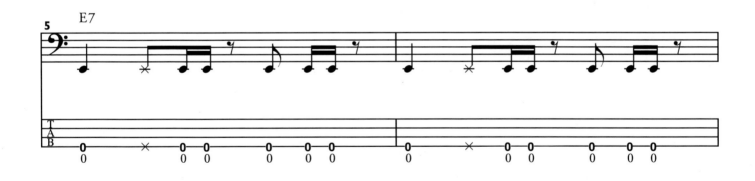

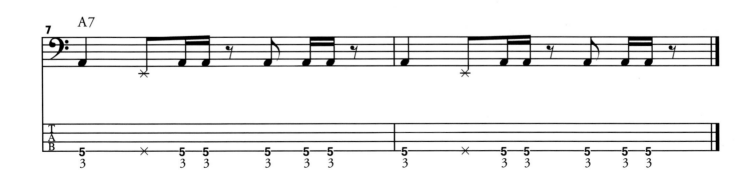

Using Roots and Octaves

Some of the most celebrated disco, soul, Motown, and funk bass lines feature chord roots and octaves. For example, on classic James Brown recordings, Bootsy Collins and others laid down memorable grooves using these tones. The tune "Car Wash" (Rose Royce) features an unmistakable bass line using these tones as well. You can play many bass lines using roots and octaves, and when you funk up the rhythm, you can create some great and memorable music.

The grooves below use roots, octaves, muted notes, and eighth- and sixteenth-note rhythms. Example 70 also includes a *slide*. A slide is accomplished by plucking a note, then sliding down or up the fretboard with the left hand. In the case below, you are sliding down the fretboard for effect; there is no specified ending point. However, sometimes you will be sliding to specific notes.

SL = Descending slide

SL = Ascending slide

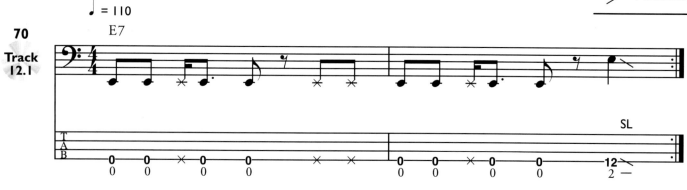

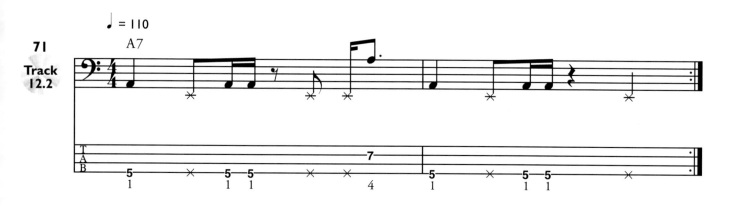

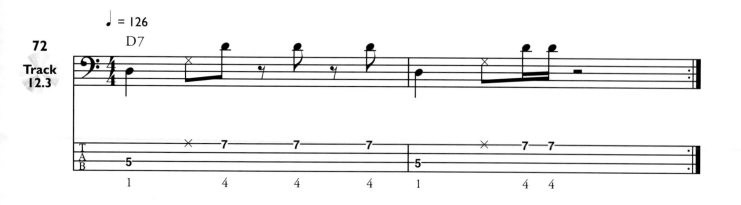

Below are more funk bass grooves using roots and octaves.
The rhythms are getting more complex, so count them
out carefully.

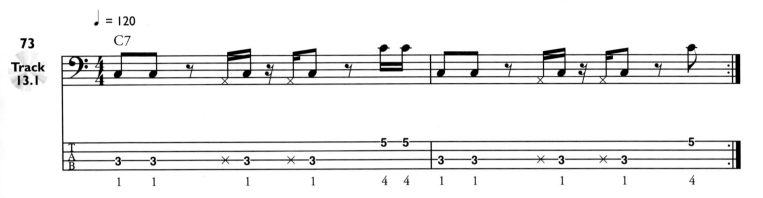

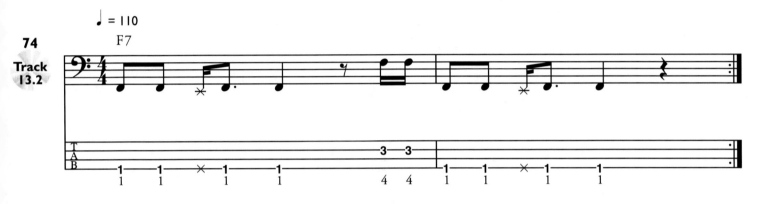

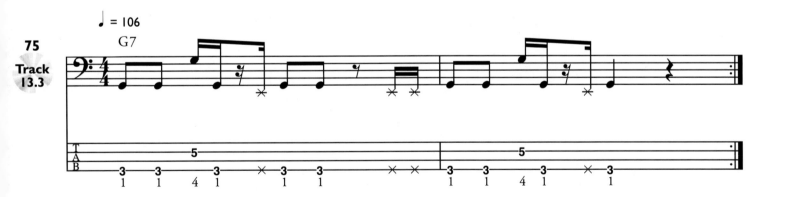

The following tune is made up entirely of the roots and octaves of the chords being played. Pay close attention to the syncopated rhythms and muted notes.

Like all of the tunes that feature a full band on the CD, the bass is panned to the left. Turn your stereo's balance control to the right and play along with the band.

Track 14 *Funk with Roots and Octaves*

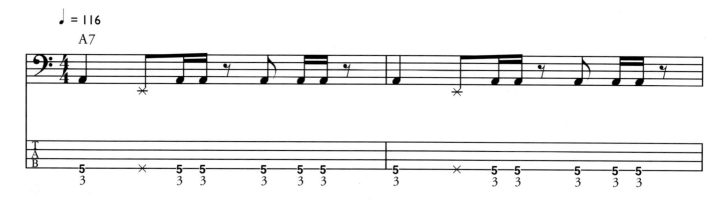

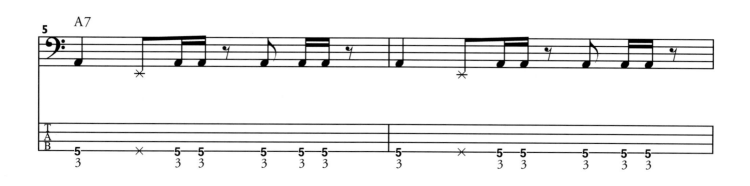

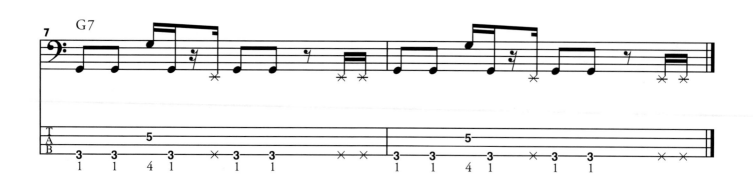

Using Roots, 5ths, and Octaves

The 5th is another chord tone that can be used to create funk bass lines. It can be used to move from the root to the octave as demonstrated in the examples below.

In the funk grooves below, count the rhythms carefully.
The ties and sixteenth rests can be very tricky.

The following tune uses the root, 5th, and octave of the chords being played. As always, count the rhythms carefully and pay attention to the muted notes.

Track 17 *One-Five-Eight-Go*

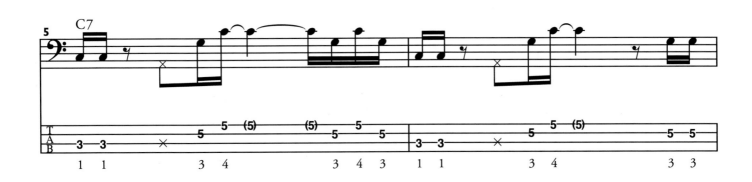

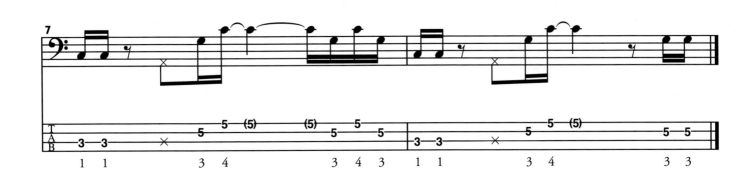

Adding 3rds and 7ths

Now, we're going to add the 3rd and 7th chord tones into the mix. This is where it starts getting tricky!

Over Dominant 7th Chords

Dominant 7th chords consist of a root, 3rd, 5th, and $\flat$7th. So, for example, when playing over a D7 chord, we will be adding an F$\sharp$ (3rd) and a C ($\flat$7th). Adding these tones while mastering the syncopated sixteenth-note rhythms will be challenging. It might be a good idea to tap the rhythms out first and then play the grooves on your bass.

Over Minor 7th Chords

Minor 7th chords consist of the root, ♭3rd, 5th, and ♭7th. So, if you were playing over an Amin7 chord, you would be adding a C (♭3rd) and a G (♭7th). In the following examples, the ♭3rd and ♭7th tones are added. Note that the number of sixteenth notes per measure is increasing. Count carefully and remember to alternate the fingers of your plucking hand.

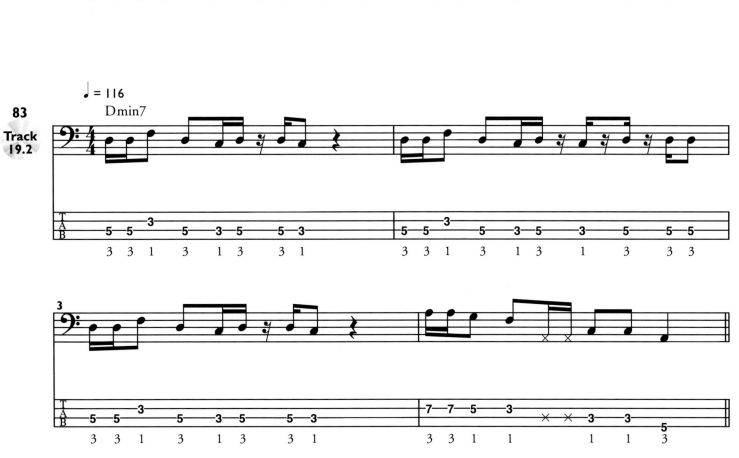

The bass line in the following tune uses the root, ♭3rd, 5th, and ♭7th of the chords being played. When listening to the CD, or playing the example yourself, notice how the sound of each chord is outlined by the notes.

Track 20 *Funky Chord Tones*

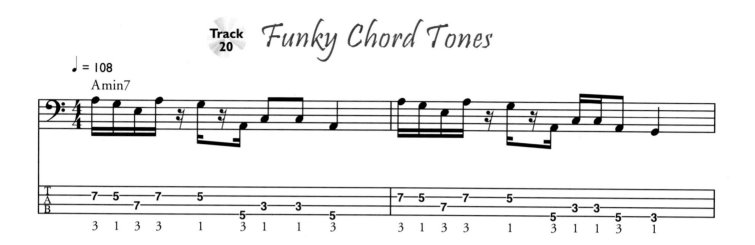

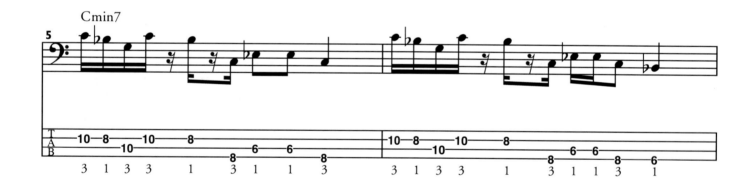

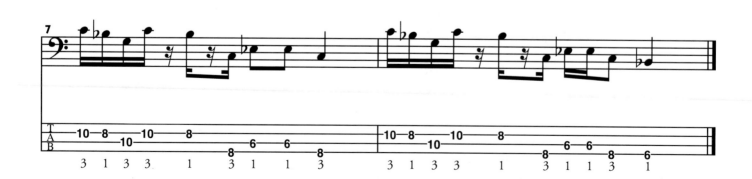

Chapter 6: Intermediate Fingerstyle Funk Grooves

In this chapter, we will be using notes from chord scales. Remember (page 33), a chord scale is simply a scale that corresponds to a particular chord. Using notes from chord scales can add more variety to your playing. Since using notes from chord scales allows you to connect chord tones with scale tones, the grooves tend to have more of a *stepwise* motion to them, meaning they have fewer interval skips. This can sometimes make it easier to play more notes (at least from a technique perspective).

Using the Mixolydian Mode

As mentioned on page 43, the dominant 7th chord is the most common type of chord in funk. The chord scale that is usually used to create bass lines over dominant 7th chords is the Mixolydian mode. You can think of this mode as a major scale with a $\flat 7$ (see page 32).

The following funk grooves consist of notes from the Mixolydian mode. So, because we are playing over an A7 in Example 84, we will be using the A Mixolydian mode (A–B–C♯–D–E–F♯–G).

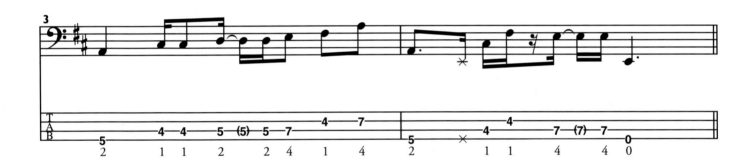

Following is a driving sixteenth-note rhythm. It's filled with
wide interval skips (like the octave jumps in measure 1)
that make it technically challenging to play. Remember, in
a groove like this, it is extremely important to alternate
the fingers of your plucking hand so you can maintain a
fast, steady rhythm.

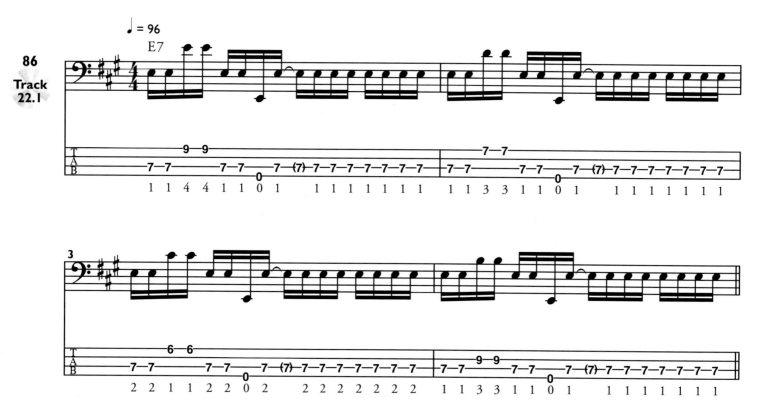

Here's one more Mixolydian groove for you to try.

The bass line in the tune below uses the Mixolydian mode over each dominant 7th chord that is played (A Mixolydian over A7 and D Mixolydian over D7). The groove consists of a one-bar pattern played four times over each chord.

Track 23 *Funky Mix*

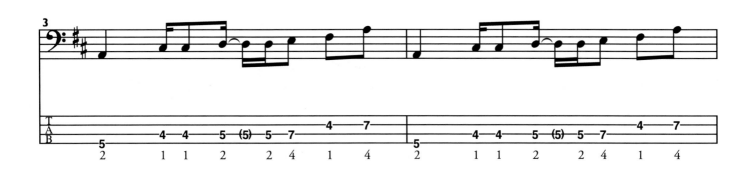

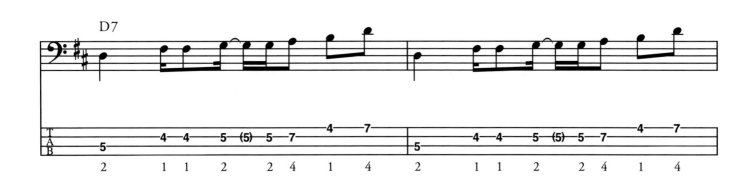

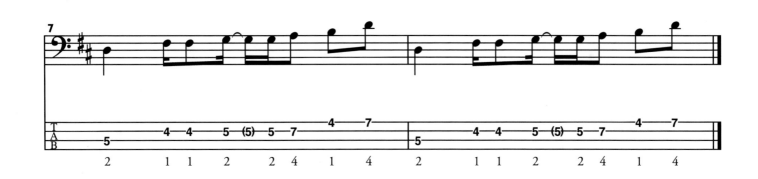

Using the Dorian Mode

Another common funk chord is the minor chord (including the minor triad and minor 7th). In many cases, the minor chord acts as the ii chord in a major key and is followed by the V chord. In fact, a common funk groove is ii min7 to V7 (refer to diatonic harmony, pages 46–47). Because minor chords often function as ii chords, a good choice for creating bass lines is the second mode of the major scale, the Dorian mode (see pages 31–33).

The funk grooves on the following pages feature the Dorian mode over each corresponding minor triad and minor 7th chord. For instance, in Example 88, we will be using the D Dorian mode over the Dmin7 chord.

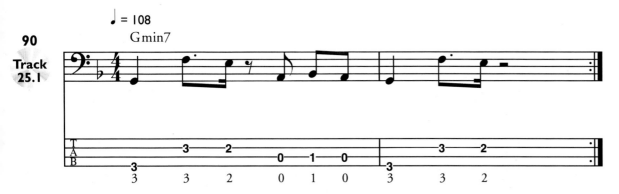

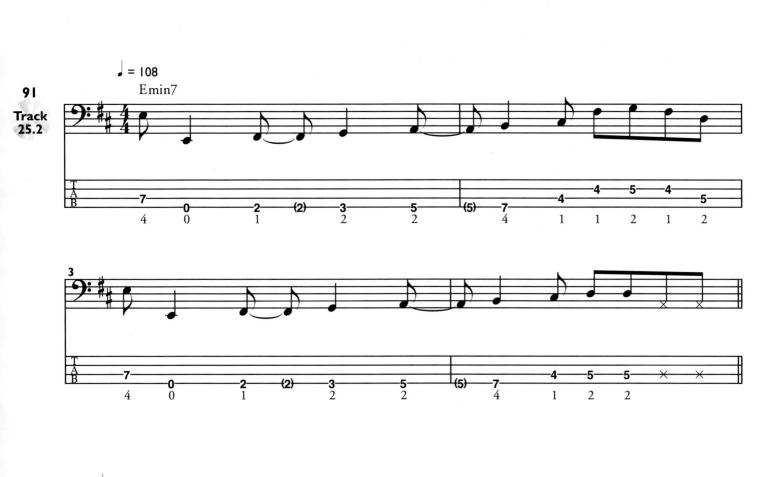

The following groove uses the Dorian mode over each chord that is played (A Dorian over Amin7 and E Dorian over Emin7). Have fun playing this along with the band on the CD.

Track 26 — *Dorian Funk*

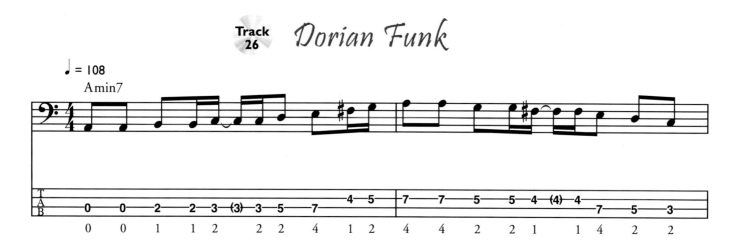

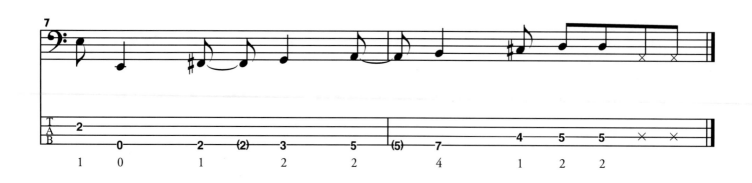

Using the Minor Pentatonic Scale

The minor pentatonic scale (see page 40) is widely used in funk, blues, and rock. The tune "Cissy Strut" by The Meters is a great example of the minor pentatonic scale used in a funk tune. The minor pentatonic scale is often used in grooves over 5 chords, minor chords, minor 7th chords, and in riff-oriented tunes. Following are examples of bass lines made up of notes from the minor pentatonic scale. When playing over an Amin7 chord, we will be using an A Minor Pentatonic, when playing over a Dmin7, we will be using a D Minor Pentatonic, etc.

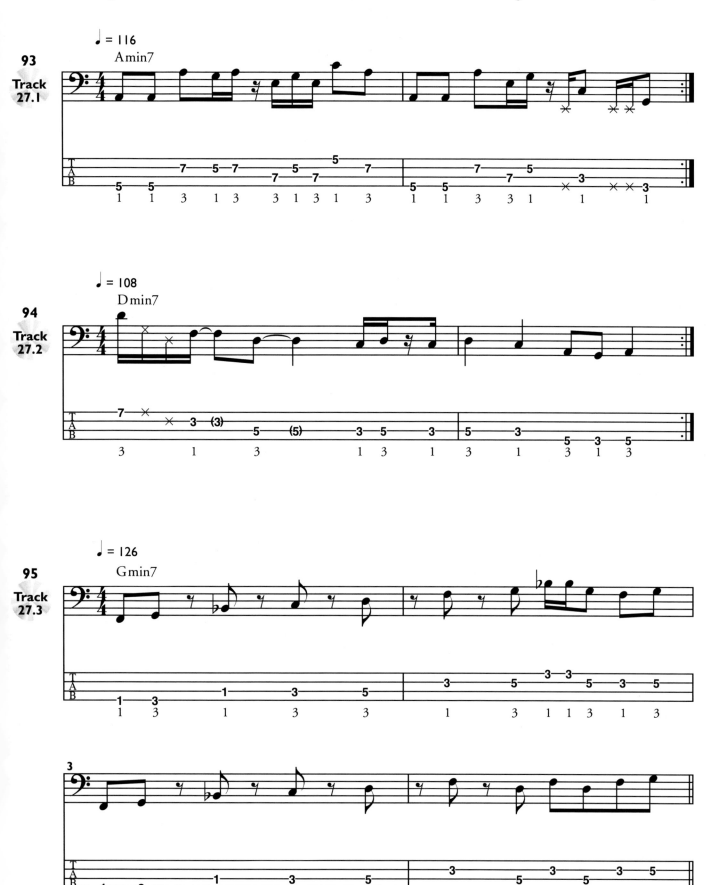

The groove in this tune uses the notes of the A Minor
Pentatonic scale.

Funk in A Minor Way

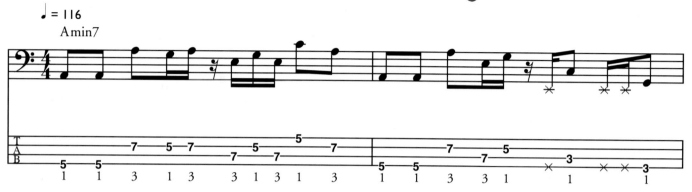

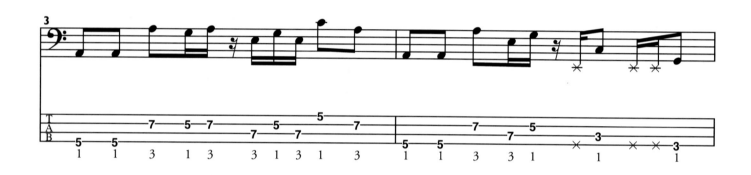

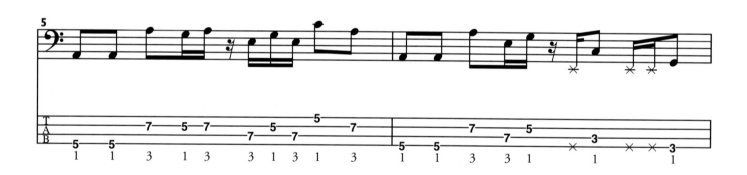

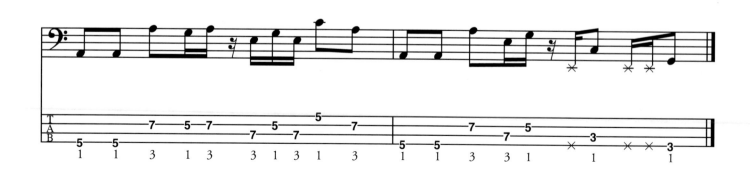

Using the Major Pentatonic Scale

The major pentatonic scale (see page 39) is often used to play grooves over major chords (including 6th chords, for example G6) and dominant 7th chords.

The grooves on this page use the notes of the major pentatonic scale. For the G and G6 chords, we will use G Major Pentatonic, and for the D7 chord, we will use D Major Pentatonic.

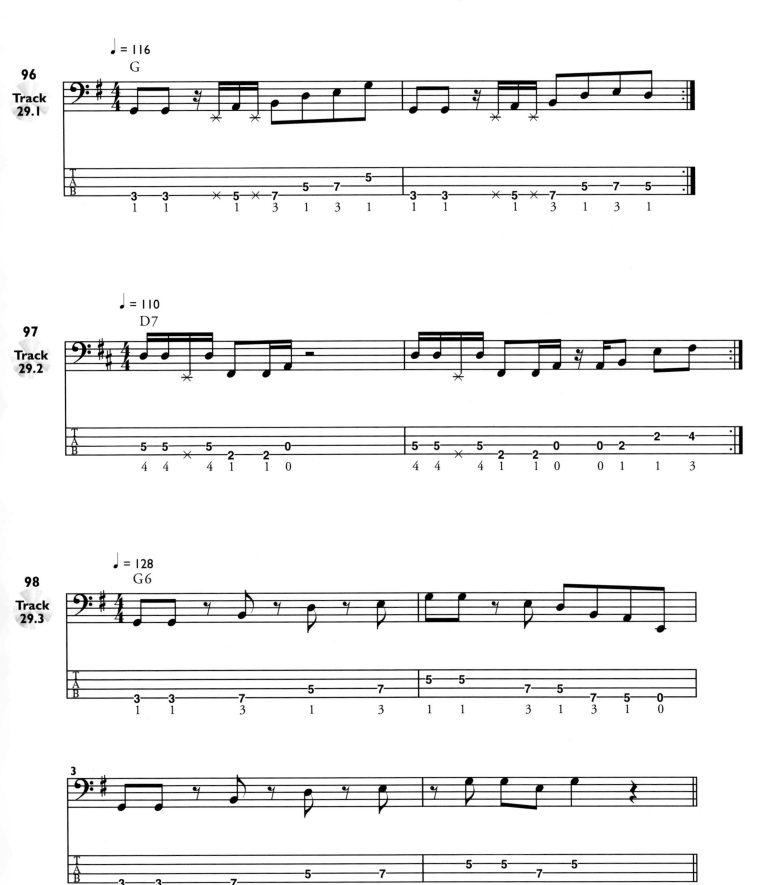

Chapter 7: Advanced Fingerstyle Funk Grooves

In this chapter, we will be using *chromatic* tones to play over one- and two-chord grooves. *Chromatic tones* are notes that do not belong to the chord scale being used; they can be used to connect scale tones and give the grooves more of a "jazzy" feel. The bass lines in this chapter also feature busier sixteenth-note rhythms with more muted notes, which will make for some seriously funky grooves.

When practicing the examples that follow, you may want to count the rhythms out and get comfortable before playing them on the bass. Also, make sure to

alternate the fingers in your plucking hand when playing sixteenth notes.

Using Chromatic Tones

Over Dominant 7th Chords

The bass lines on this page are all over Dominant 7th chords. They are composed of the Mixolydian mode (E Mixolydian over E7, etc.) and chromatic tones.

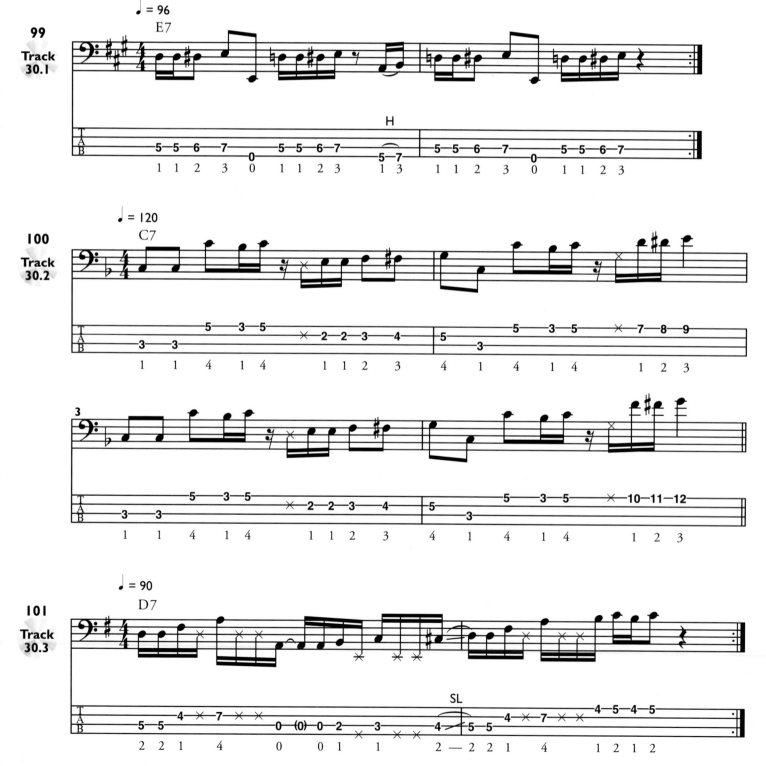

Over Minor Chords

The bass lines on this page are over minor chords, and they are built using the Dorian mode and chromatic tones.

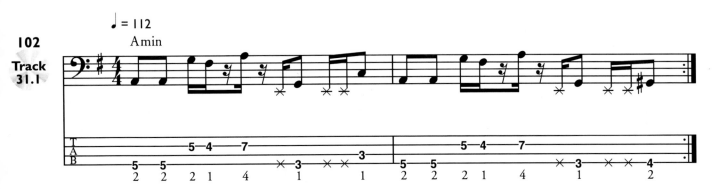

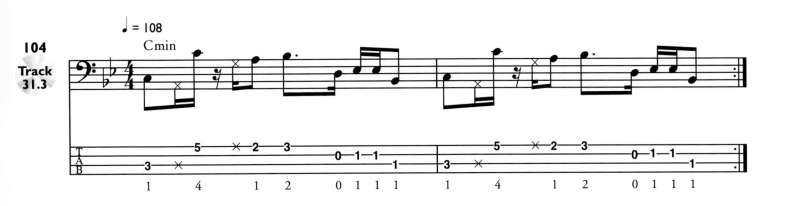

The following bass line is built using the C Mixolydian mode
and chromatic tones.

Track 32 *Chromatic Funk*

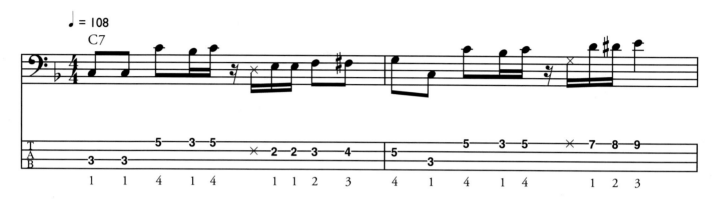

Over Two-Chord Grooves

Up to this point, all of the funk grooves you have played have been written on one chord. Remember, the emphasis in funk is on rhythm and the "pocket," and not complex harmony. While it is true that many funk tunes consist of only one chord, you'll also find tunes and jams that use two chords.

In two-chord funk, it is common to find a minor 7th chord (the ii chord) followed by a dominant 7th chord (the V chord). Because the minor 7th functions as a ii chord, the bassist applies the Dorian mode over this chord. Because the dominant 7th chord functions as a V chord, the Mixolydian mode will be applied over this chord.

When this type of ii–V progression is used in funk, bassists will sometimes play the same rhythmic pattern over the two chords, adjusting the notes from Dorian to Mixolydian when the chords change. In other words, you would start your pattern on the root of the ii chord using the Dorian mode, then play the pattern starting on the root of the V chord making sure to use just the notes of the Mixolydian mode.

The first two grooves on this page feature the ii–V progression. Example 107 is over two dominant chords (D Mixolydian is played over D7 and G Mixolydian is played over G7). All of the grooves that follow feature chromatic tones.

The following examples are over ii–V progressions.
Example 108 is in the style of the Tower of Power tune
"What Is Hip?"

The next example is in the style of another song with a
funky bass line, Queen's "Another One Bites the Dust."

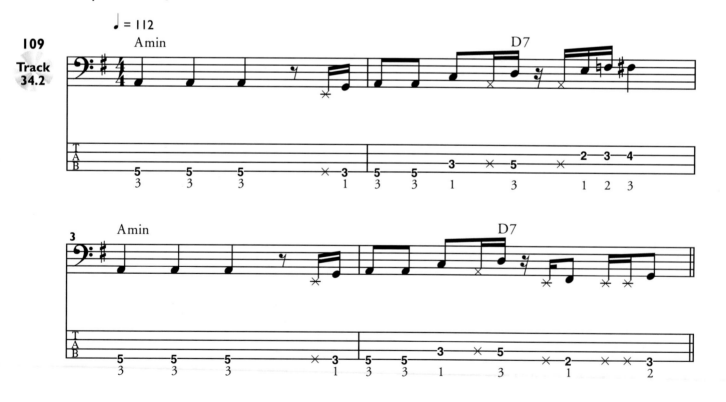

The following is a two-chord funk groove featuring a ii–V
progression and chromatic tones.

Track
35
Funky Two-Chord

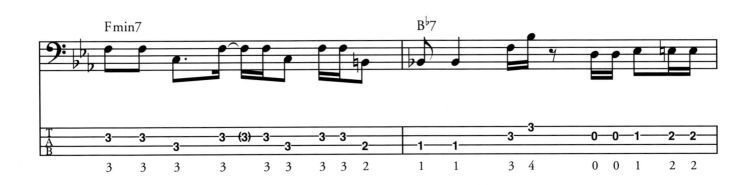

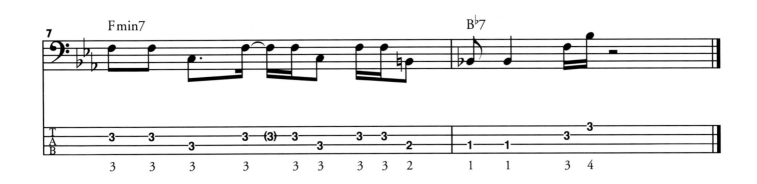

Chapter 8: The Slap & Pop Style

The slap & pop style of bass playing was developed by Larry Graham, best known for his work in the 1970s with Sly & the Family Stone and Graham Central Station. The technique has evolved from the 1970s to the present. Players like Bootsy Collins, Louis Johnson, Flea, Meshell Ndegeocello, Marc King, Marcus Miller, Stanley Clarke, and Victor Wooten have all contributed to the development of slap & pop.

The slap & pop style has a percussive quality produced by using two main techniques: slapping the string with the right-hand thumb and popping the string with the right-hand 1st finger. The style also makes use of muted notes, hammer-ons, pull-offs, and slides. Below is a chart featuring brief explanations for some of these techniques and the abbreviations that appear in the music. The abbreviations appear above both the standard music notation staff and the TAB staff.

Slap & Pop Techniques	
S	**Thumb slap:** Strike the string with your right-hand thumb. The string should make a percussive sound as it strikes the fretboard.
P	**Pop:** Pluck, or "pop," the string with the 1st finger of your right hand. The string will snap back and strike the fretboard, creating a sharp, percussive sound.
H	**Hammer-on:** Play a note, then play a higher-pitched note on the same string by "hammering" onto the fret with another left-hand finger. Do not use your right hand for the second note; the sound comes from the left hand alone.
PO	**Pull-off:** A pull-off is the opposite of a hammer-on. Play a note, then play a lower-pitched note on the same string by quickly pulling your left-hand finger off the fret. Do not use your right hand for the second note; the sound comes from the left hand alone.

More detailed explanations of the techniques above will follow. In the first section, we will cover the "slapping" aspect of the slap & pop style.

The Slap Technique

The slap technique is achieved by striking the string with your thumb. This causes the string to "slap" against the fretboard, creating a percussive effect.

When using the slap technique, a softer, or lighter, attack usually produces a better tone. It also allows for more *dynamics* (how loud or soft you play). This is true for the pop technique as well, which we will be looking at in the next section.

The angle at which you hold your hand when slapping is one of personal preference. The pictures below show two common slapping positions. Most players prefer slap position 1 because holding the hand this way makes it easier to follow the slap with a pop. However, try both and use whichever way works best for you.

Slap position 1.

Slap position 2.

Listen to Track 36 to hear how the slap technique is supposed to sound. Then, try it yourself using just the open 4th string.

110

Track 36

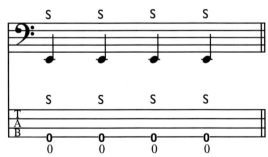

Slap Technique Exercises

The following exercises will help you get comfortable with the slap technique. Concentrate on producing a good tone from each note. Also, experiment with the angle of your thumb and how hard you slap the string. You will be slapping muted notes as well as fretted notes. The right-hand technique for both is the same (the muting is accomplished by the left hand).

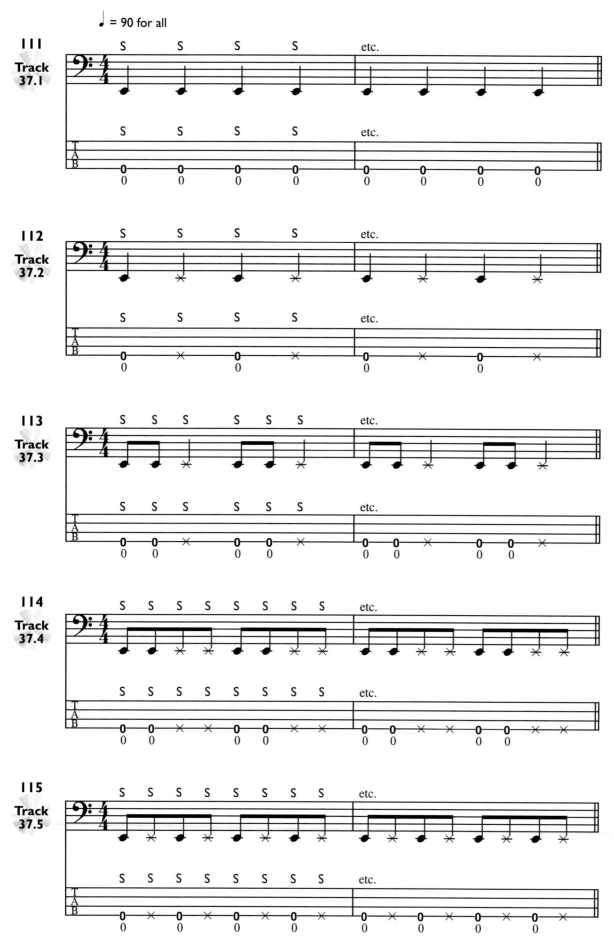

The exercises below are similar to those on the previous page except they are played on the 3rd string. Slapping the 3rd string can be tricky at first because you have to strike the string while avoiding the 2nd and 4th strings. Again, experiment with the angle of your thumb and how hard you slap the string.

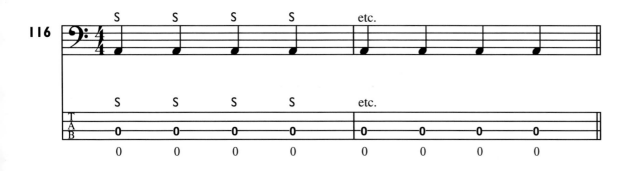

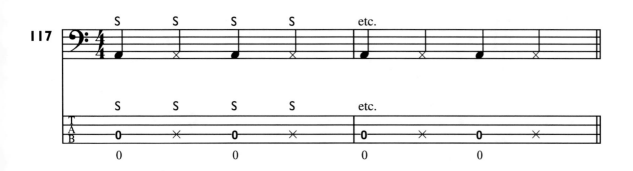

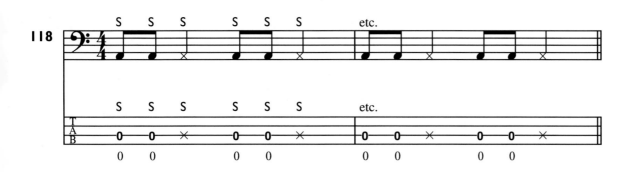

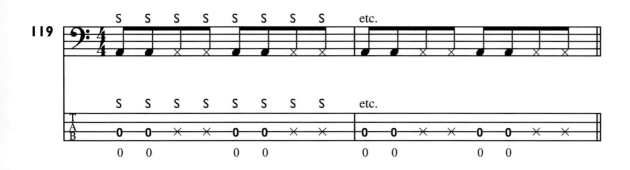

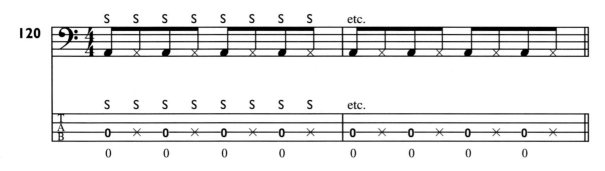

The Pop Technique

To perform the pop technique, place the index finger of the right hand underneath the string (usually the 1st or 2nd string), then pull the string away from the fretboard and let it go, allowing it to snap back against the frets. This produces a very percussive sound, more so than the slap. Again, you can achieve this technique by holding your hand at one of two angles (see pictures below); try both and use whichever works best for you.

Pop position 1.

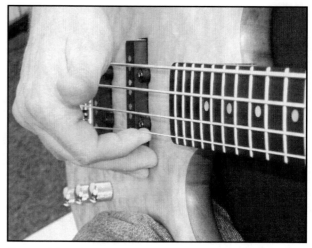

Pop position 2.

Listen to Track 38 to hear how the pop technique is supposed to sound. Then, try it yourself, using just the open 1st string.

121

Track 38

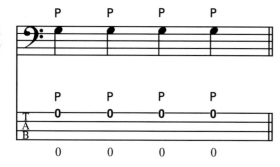

Slap & Pop Technique Exercises

The exercises below combine the slap and pop techniques, and they will help you get used to popping on the 1st string. Experiment with the angle of the 1st finger when plucking the string to see what works best for you.

Also, you will be popping muted notes as well as fretted notes. The right-hand technique for both is the same (the muting is accomplished by the left hand).

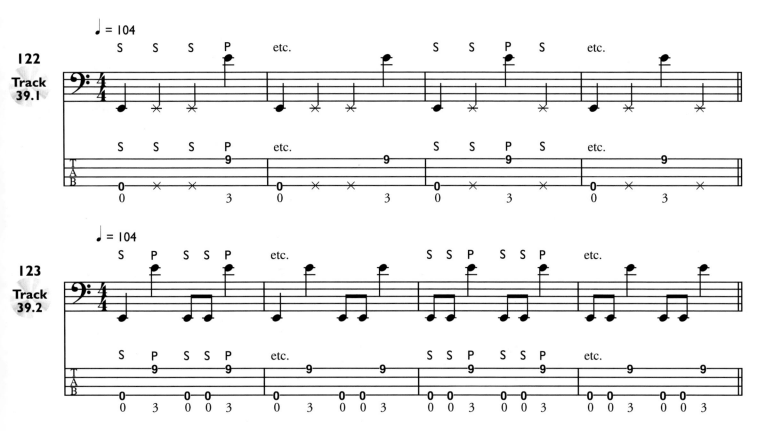

The following example is played using triplets (see page 10).
Triplets are counted: 1–&–a, 2–&–a, 3–&–a, 4–&–a.

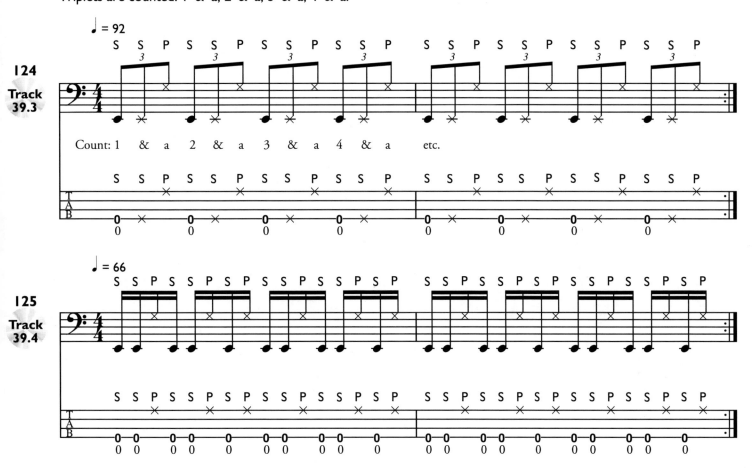

The exercises below are similar to those on the previous page except you will now be popping the 2nd string. It can be a little tricky to pop the 2nd string because you need to get your right-hand 1st finger in between the 1st and 3rd strings. Experiment with the angle of your 1st finger when playing through these exercises.

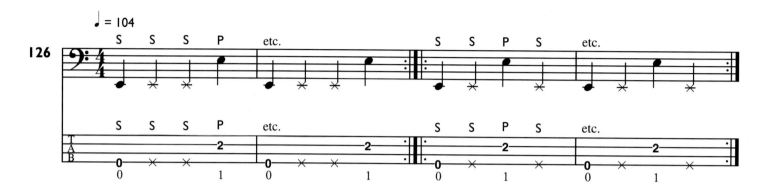

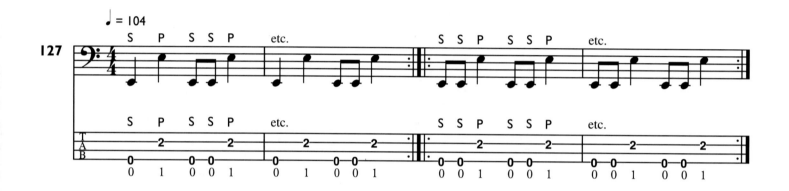

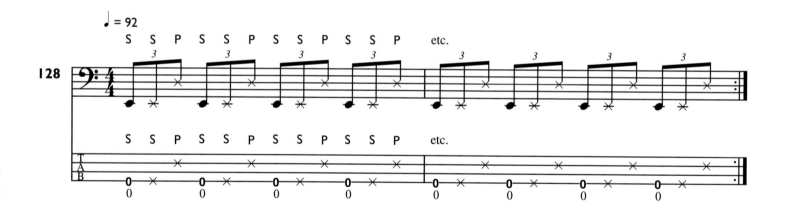

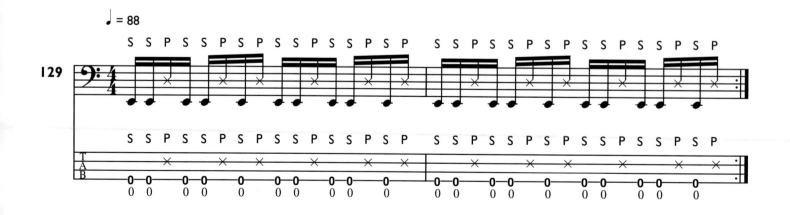

Slapping the 3rd String

In the exercises below, you will be popping the 1st string and slapping the 3rd string. As you learned on page 79, the challenge is to avoid the 2nd and 4th strings while executing a clean slap on the 3rd string. Try playing these exercises slowly at first to make sure you are comfortable with this technique.

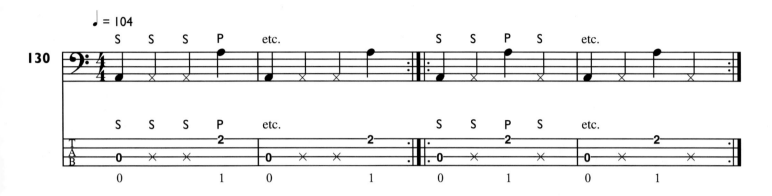

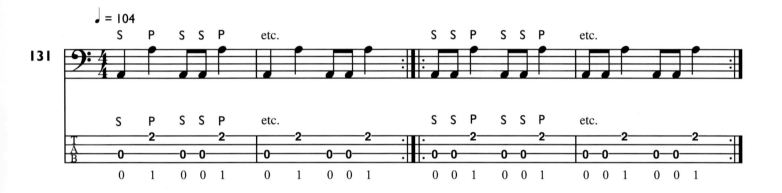

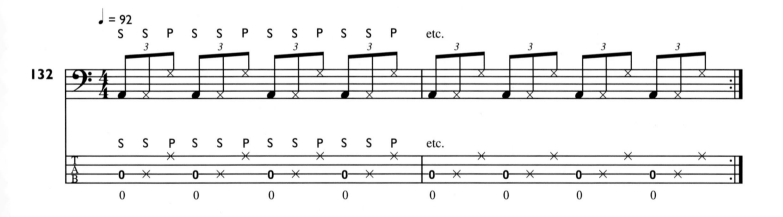

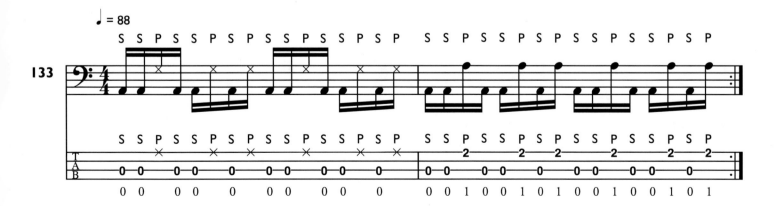

The Hammer-On

The hammer-on is a left-hand technique frequently used in the slap & pop style. It is notated with a *slur,* which is a curved line over or under a group of notes. The slur indicates the notes are to be played *legato* (smooth and flowing).

As mentioned on page 76, a hammer-on is achieved by playing a note, then playing a higher-pitched note on the same string by "hammering" onto the fret with another left-hand finger. We will be using hammer-ons in conjunction with both slaps and pops.

Below is an example of a slap followed by a hammer-on.

Here's an example of an open-string slap followed by a hammer-on.

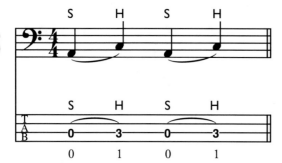

The following exercise features slaps, hammer-ons, quarter notes, and eighth notes.

Hammer-On Exercises

Below are hammer-on exercises on all four strings. Strive for an even volume on all the notes, and make sure your tempo is steady and consistent.

Hammer-Ons with Quarter Notes

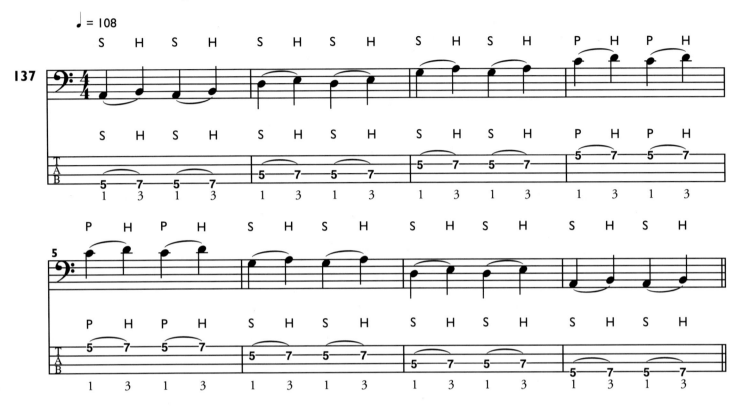

Hammer-Ons with Eighth Notes

Hammer-Ons with Sixteenth Notes

The Pull-Off

The pull-off is another left-hand technique frequently used in the slap & pop style. It is notated with a slur and, as mentioned on page 76, it is achieved by playing a note, then sounding a lower-pitched note on the same string by quickly pulling your left-hand finger off the fret.

We will be using pull-offs in conjunction with slaps, but more frequently with pops. Try the following examples to start getting used to this technique. Remember to strive for an even volume between notes, and keep a steady tempo.

Pull-Offs with Quarter Notes

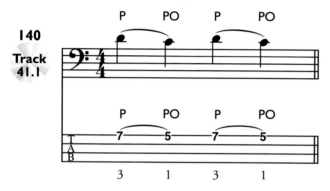

Pull-Offs with Eighth Notes

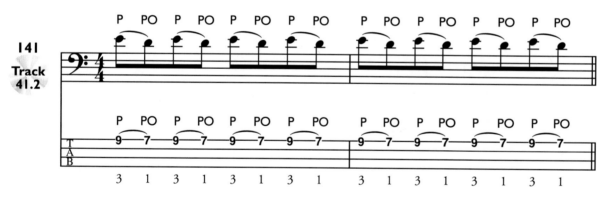

Pull-Offs and Hammer-Ons with Sixteenth Notes

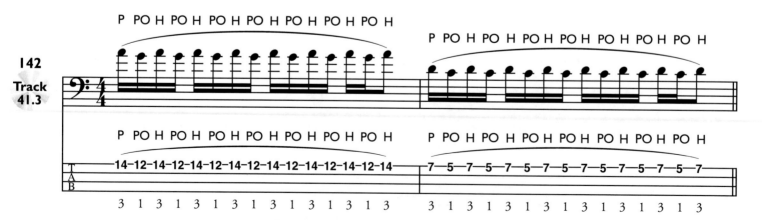

Popped Double Stops

A *double stop* is two notes played simultaneously on a single instrument. Double stops are often used in the slap & pop style. It is common to slap a note, then follow it with a popped double stop consisting of the 5th and octave above the slapped note.

In the example below, the D note on the 3rd string is slapped, and the A and D notes on the 2nd and 1st strings are popped simultaneously using the 1st and 2nd fingers.

P1 = Pop with the 1st finger of the right hand.

P2 = Pop with the 2nd finger of the right hand.

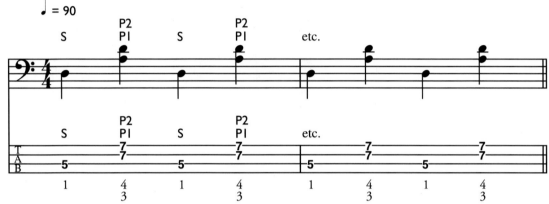

Double Popping

A *double pop* is two consecutive popped notes played on two adjacent strings, usually the 2nd and 1st strings. The double pop can be executed in a triplet, as in the example below.

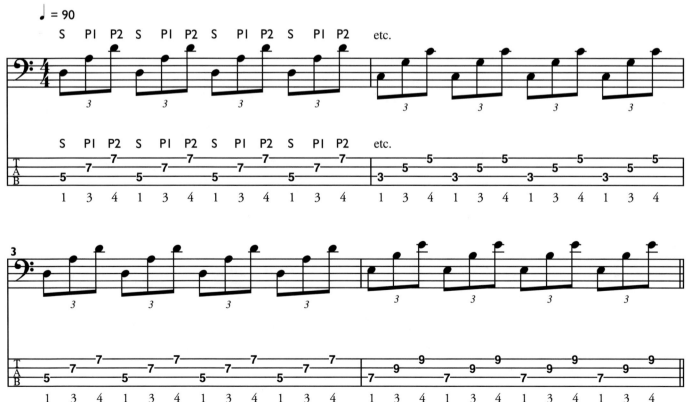

Double Thumping

Double thumping is a relatively new technique popularized by Victor Wooten. It consists of using the thumb for both downstrokes and upstrokes, much like using a pick. When playing downstrokes, the thumb should play "through the string" in a downward motion. This will set up your thumb to play an upstroke, which is accomplished by striking the string with your thumb in a upward motion.

The double thumping technique is often used to play rhythms with lots of notes and faster tempos. As with picking, you can play faster rhythms alternating downstrokes and upstrokes, rather than just using all downstrokes. The challenge is to get an even sound with both downstrokes and upstrokes. Although this technique can be used to play both muted and unmuted notes, in this book, it is only used on muted notes. Below are some exercises to get you started.

T1 = Thumb downstroke
T2 = Thumb upstroke

The following example is in $\frac{6}{8}$ time, which means there are six beats per measure with the eighth note receiving the beat. Though you can count each beat (1, 2, 3, 4, 5, 6, etc.), it is more common to count as shown below.

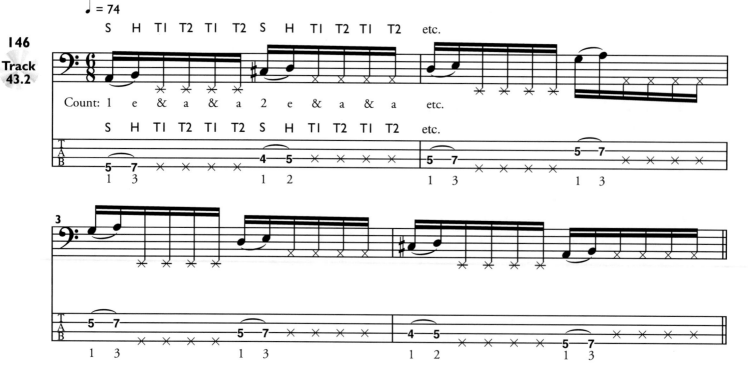

Muted Hammer-Ons

As we learned on pages 84–85, we can use the hammer-on to sound a fretted note by hammering a left-hand finger onto the fretboard. We can also use this technique to cause muted notes to sound.

The *muted hammer-on* technique is achieved by plucking a muted note, then sharply bringing two or more left-hand fingers onto the string without pressing it to the fretboard. This results in a percussive sound similar to that of a muted note.

To get you used to the muted hammer-on technique, we'll start with some fretted hammer-ons. Play the following exercise.

147
Track 44.1

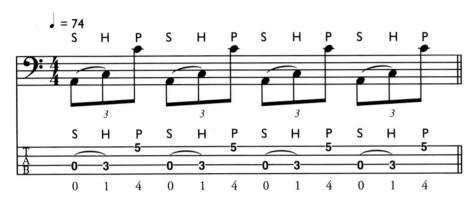

The following example is similar to the one above except the first two notes of each triplet are replaced with muted notes. So, you will be plucking the first muted note of each triplet, then hammering-on with your left hand to sound the next muted note, then popping the third note of each triplet.

148
Track 44.2

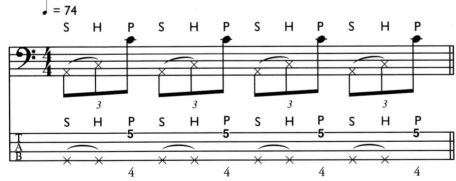

As with all of these advanced techniques, the muted hammer-on should be used in the right musical situations. Always try to use the technique in a musical fashion; don't crowbar it into a song just to show off.

Chapter 9: Starter Slap & Pop Funk Grooves

Now that we have examined the different techniques used in the slap & pop style, let's apply them to some funk grooves. This chapter uses the slap technique only.

Using the Root

As with the fingerstyle funk bass lines we played earlier, we'll begin with starter slap grooves using the roots of the chords being played. The funk grooves below use chord roots and the slap technique. Note the use of muted notes.

Note: When playing in the slap & pop style, the left-hand fingerings might be slightly different than if you were playing fingerstyle. The reason for this is that certain fingers of the left hand are being used to mute strings. Keep in mind that all fingerings in this book are just suggestions. You may find fingerings that are more comfortable for you—don't be afraid to experiment!

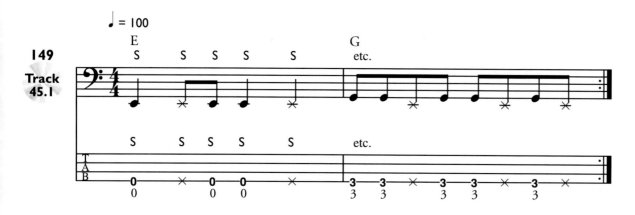

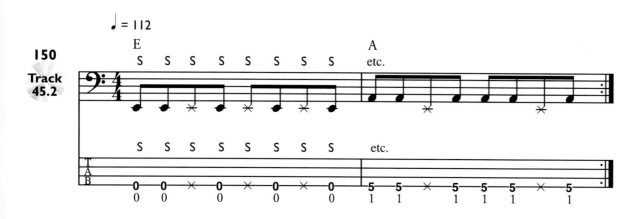

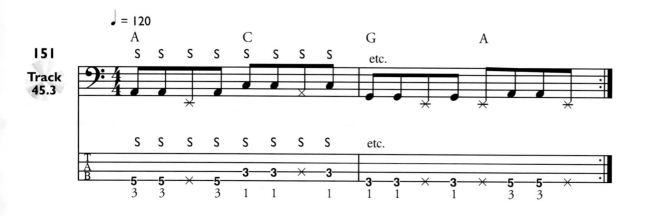

Dominant 7th Grooves

The slap-style funk grooves on this page are played over dominant 7th chords. Remember, the tones of the dominant 7th chord are 1, 3, 5, and ♭7. The sound of each chord is outlined by using these chord tones. Note that there are some slapped notes on the 2nd string.

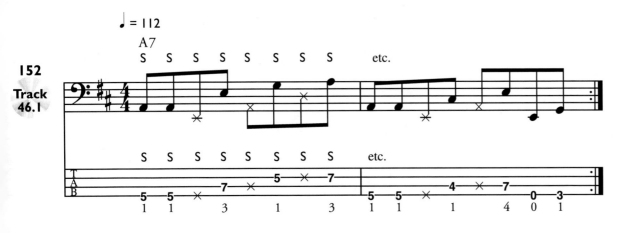

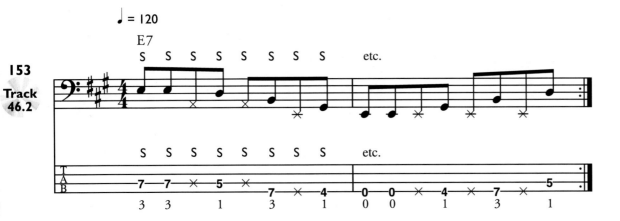

In the following two-chord funk groove, we will be using the tones of the A7 chord in the first measure and the tones of the D7 chord in the second measure.

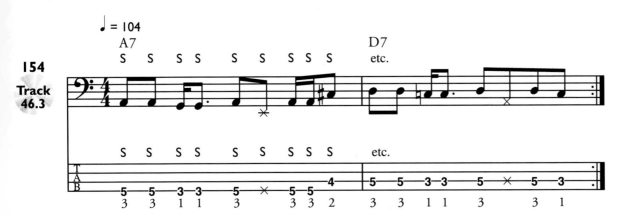

Minor 7th Grooves

The slap style funk grooves on this page are over minor 7th chords. Remember, the tones of the minor 7th chord are 1, ♭3, 5, and ♭7. The sound of each chord is outlined by using these chord tones.

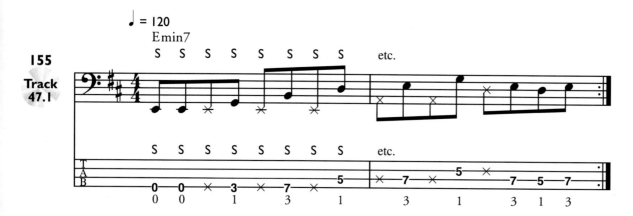

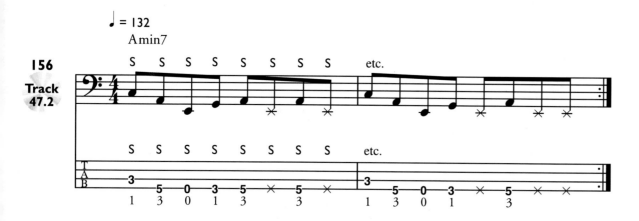

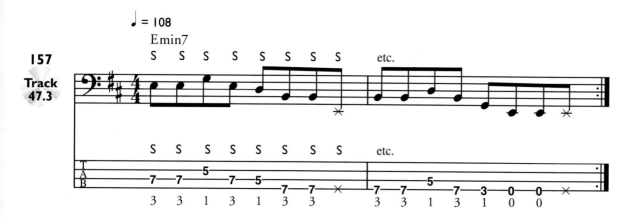

Mixolydian and Dorian Grooves

The slap-style grooves on this page are made using notes from the appropriate chord scales. The chord scale to play over dominant 7th chords is the Mixolydian mode, and the chord scale to play over minor 7th chords is the Dorian mode.

Using the Mixolydian Mode

The following two funk grooves use the notes of the Mixolydian mode. Example 158 uses A Mixolydian and Example 159 uses G Mixolydian. Remember, the Mixolydian mode is like a major scale with a ♭7.

Using the Dorian Mode

The following two funk grooves use the notes of the Dorian mode. Remember, the Dorian mode consists of scale degrees 1, 2, ♭3, 4, 5, 6, and ♭7.

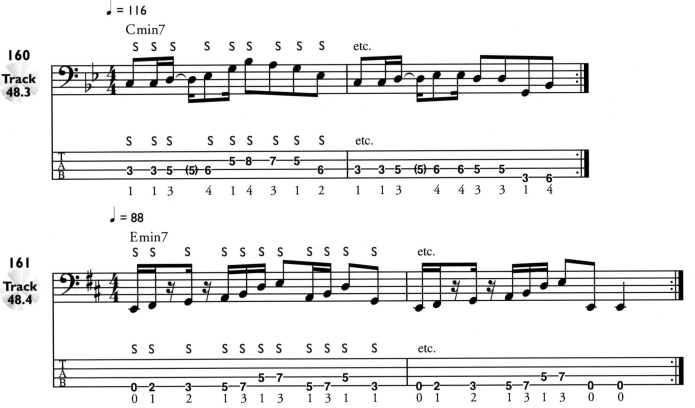

Chapter 10: Intermediate Slap & Pop Funk Grooves

Now, let's move on to more challenging funk bass lines combining the slap & pop techniques. When playing the grooves in this chapter, remember to stop notes from ringing after you have played them so that no unwanted string noise occurs. Remember also to play with a light touch, as this will give you more control over your sound and make it easier to avoid string noise.

Using Chord Tones

Although funk is primarily a rhythmic music, great grooves can also outline the harmony of a tune, and this is done by using chord tones. The intermediate funk grooves below are made up of chord tones belonging to the chords being played. Example 162 outlines the sound of the Gmin7 chord in the first measure and C7 in the second measure.

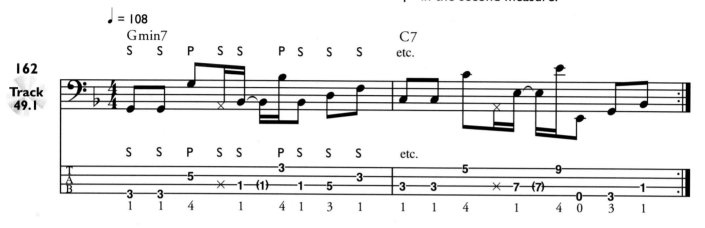

The groove below outlines the sound of the D Minor 7th chord.

The following groove outlines the sound of the E Minor 7th chord.

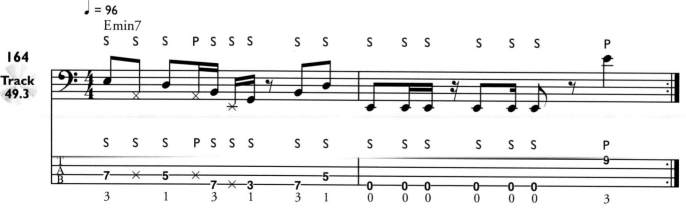

Using the Dorian Mode

Now, we will play slap & pop grooves using the Dorian mode. By now, you know that the Dorian mode is the chord scale used over minor 7th chords. Remember, chord scales give you a greater variety of notes from which to choose and they also enable you to connect chord tones.

Play the following Dorian grooves with a light touch and remember to count the rhythms carefully.

165
Track 50.1

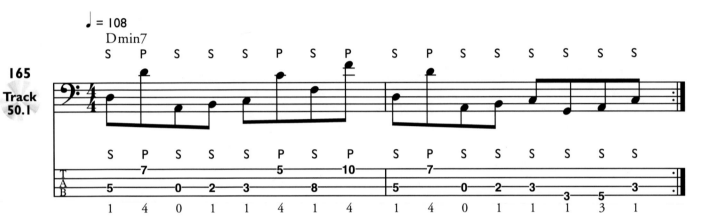

166
Track 50.2

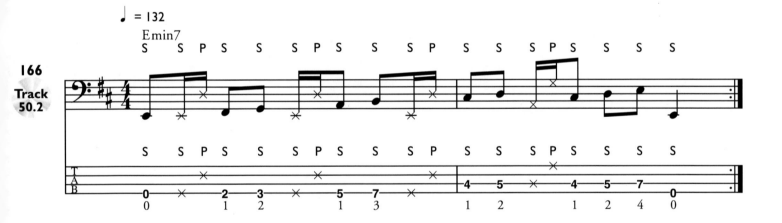

167
Track 50.3

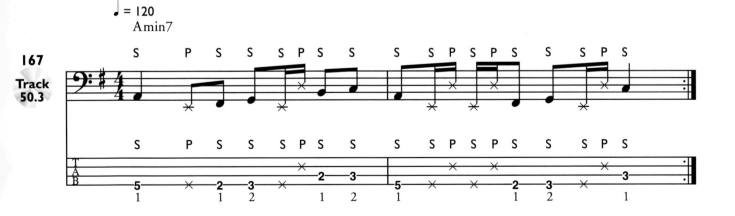

Using Chromatic Tones

The funk grooves on this page include chromatic tones, which can be used to connect scale tones. They can also be used to approach the root note of a new chord by a half step or whole step. When used in this way, they are called *approach tones*.

Example 168 uses chromatic tones on the last note of each chord to approach the first note of each new chord by a half step. Play this one very slowly at first until you are comfortable with the rhythms.

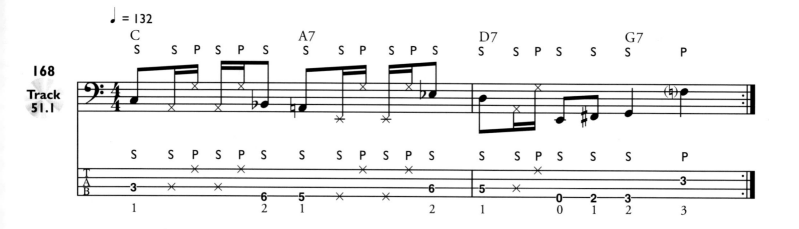

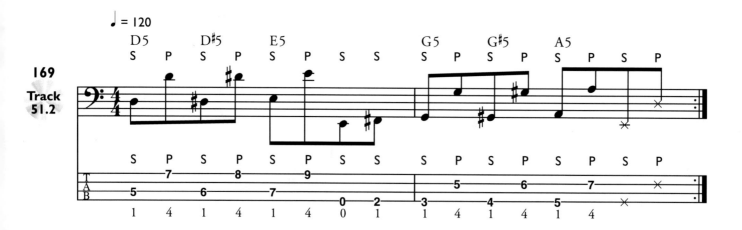

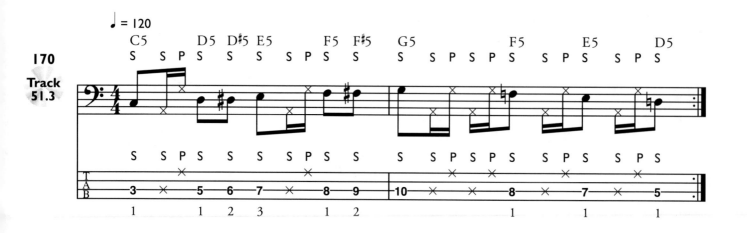

Using Hammer-Ons and Pull-Offs

The following grooves use hammer-ons and pull-offs. As all of the different techniques and concepts are combined, it may take longer to master the examples. Count carefully and maintain a steady tempo.

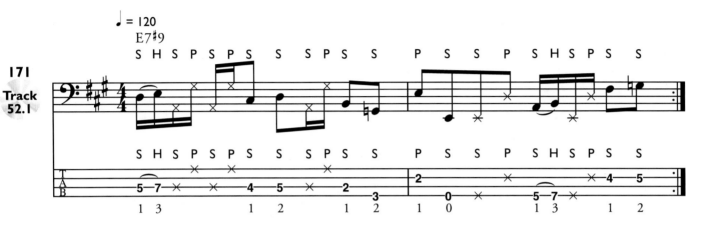

In the next example, notice the sixteenth-note triplet in the second measure. This divides one half of a beat equally among three sixteenth notes. (Normally, two sixteenth notes last for a half a beat.)

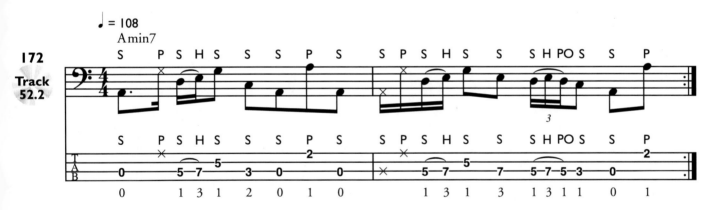

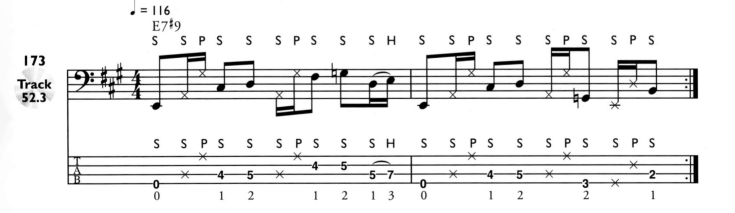

Here are some more grooves featuring hammer-ons
and pull-offs.

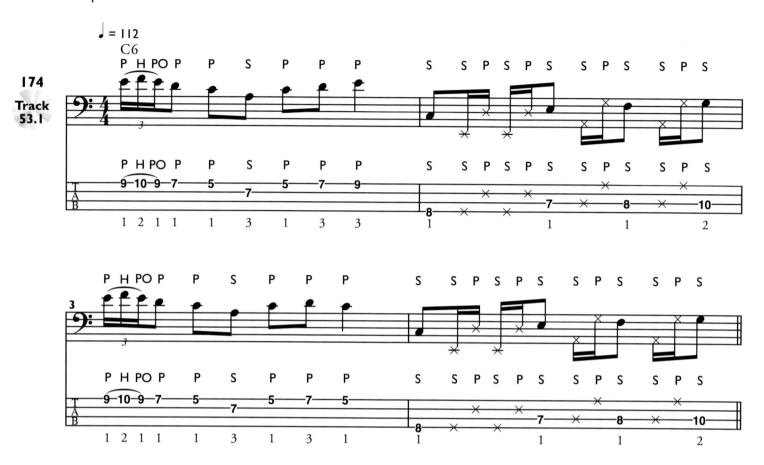

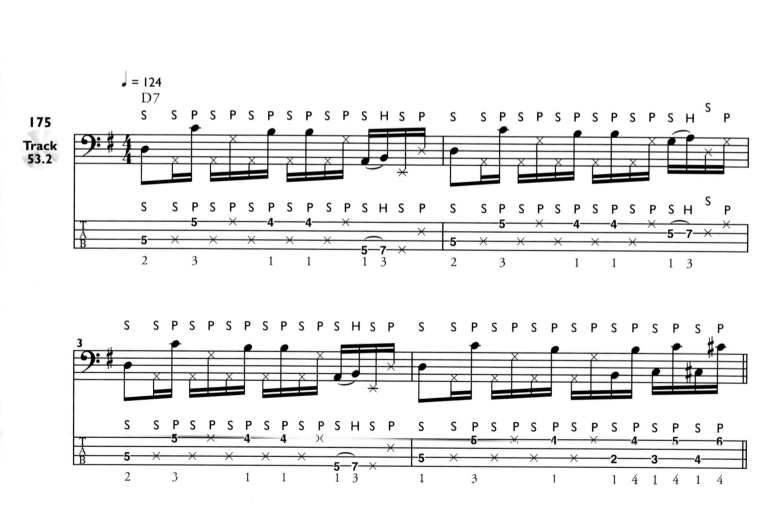

The following bass line is derived from the B Phrygian mode. Remember (page 31), the Phrygian mode is the third mode of the major scale, so B Phrygian is the third mode of the G Major scale. Notice the exotic sound created by this mode.

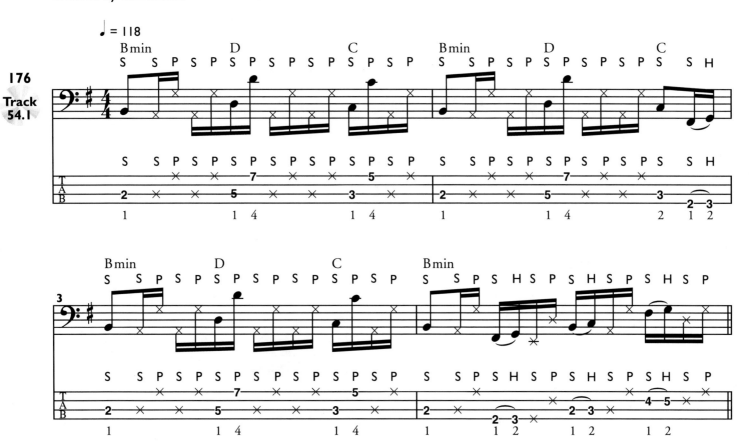

Now, check out this dominant 7th groove.

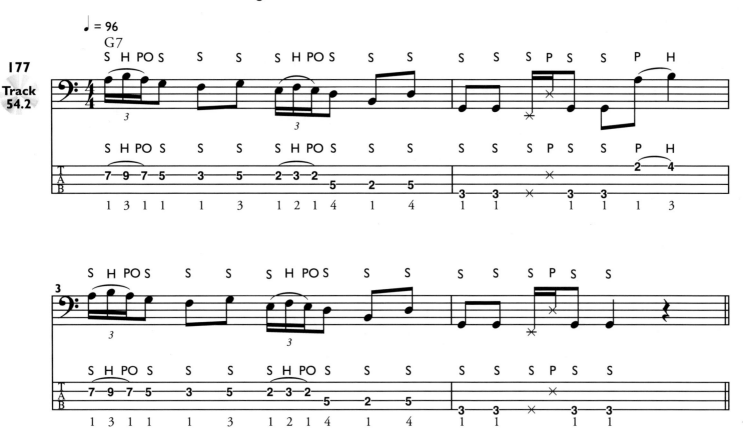

The following tune features the slap, pop, and hammer-on techniques. There are many sixteenth notes in this groove so play it very slowly at first and count carefully.

Remember to dampen the strings for muted notes and use a light touch for the slap & pop techniques.

Hammer It Home

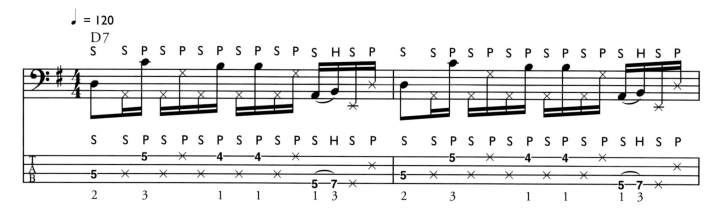

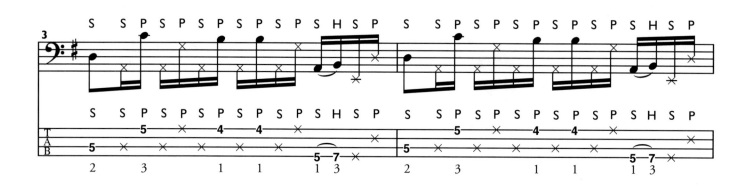

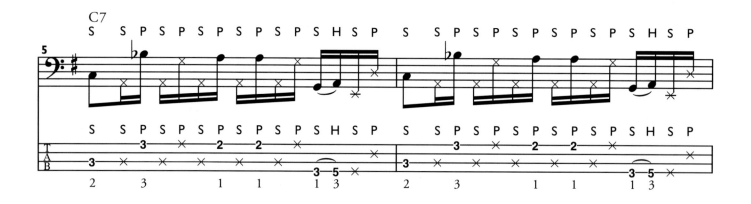

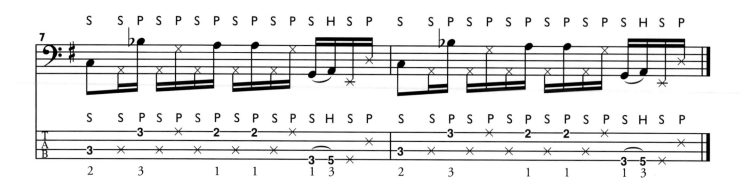

Chapter 11: Advanced Slap & Pop Funk Grooves

In this chapter, we'll continue our slap & pop explorations with more hammer-ons and pull-offs. Then, we'll play grooves that feature slides, double thumping, popped double stops, and double popping. With this much going on, be sure to practice the examples very slowly at first. Execute the techniques as cleanly as possible at a slow speed, then increase the tempo. (Even at slow speeds, these grooves are mighty funky!)

The examples on the next two pages feature hammer-ons and pull-offs.

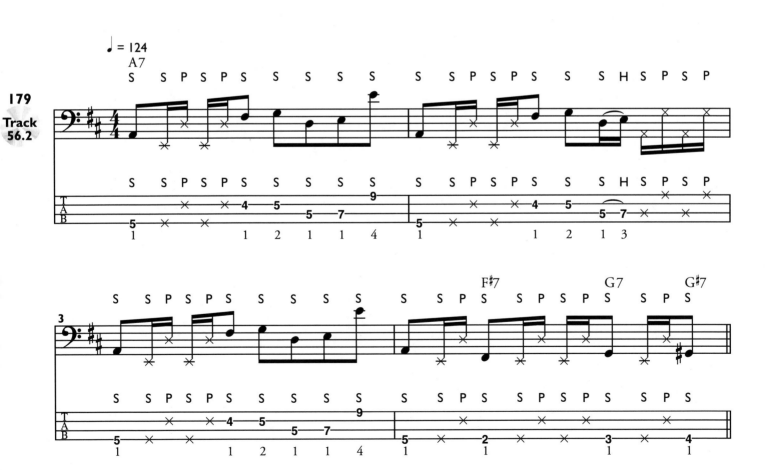

The examples on this page are over two-chord funk grooves (ii–V progressions). They use chord tones, chord scale tones, and approach tones.

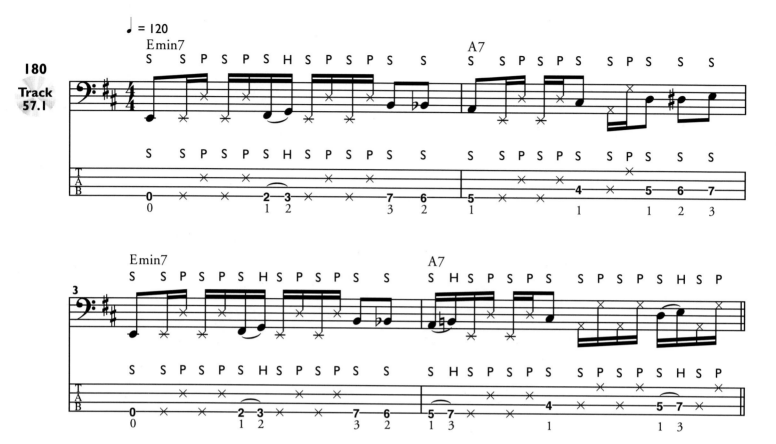

Double Thumping Grooves

It's time for some grooves featuring the double thumping technique. Remember (page 88), this technique consists of alternating downstrokes and upstrokes with the thumb, much like a pick.

In the bass lines that follow, focus on alternating the thumb downstrokes and upstrokes evenly and with equal volume.

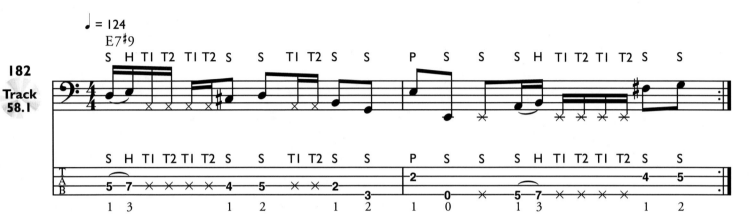

Note the muted sixteenth-note triplets in bar 2 of the following example. Muted triplets add a great percussive effect to this groove. Before trying the entire example, play through the triplets very slowly to make sure you are muting the strings effectively and not getting any string noise. Once you are comfortable with this, try the entire groove.

Here's another cool double thumping groove. The bass line is built from the notes of the A Dorian mode.

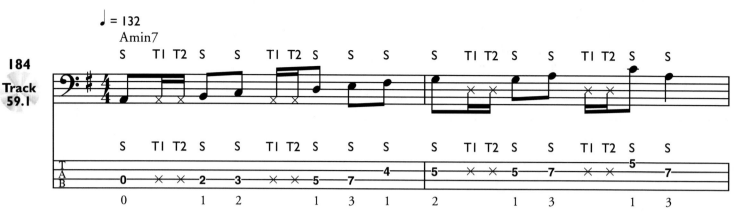

Below is another bass line featuring muted sixteenth-note triplets.

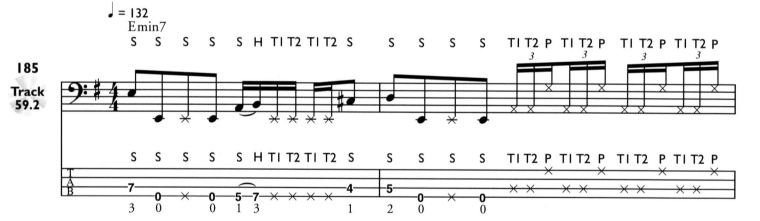

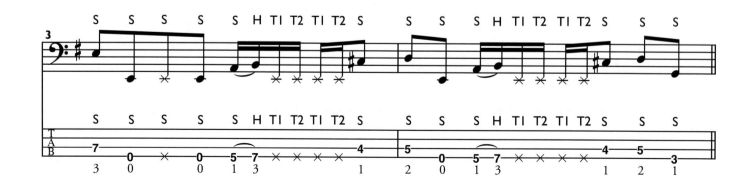

Double Thumping Grooves with Popped Double Stops

The following groove features double thumping and popped double stops (see page 87). It's played over two ii–V progressions (Amin–D7 and Gmin–C7).

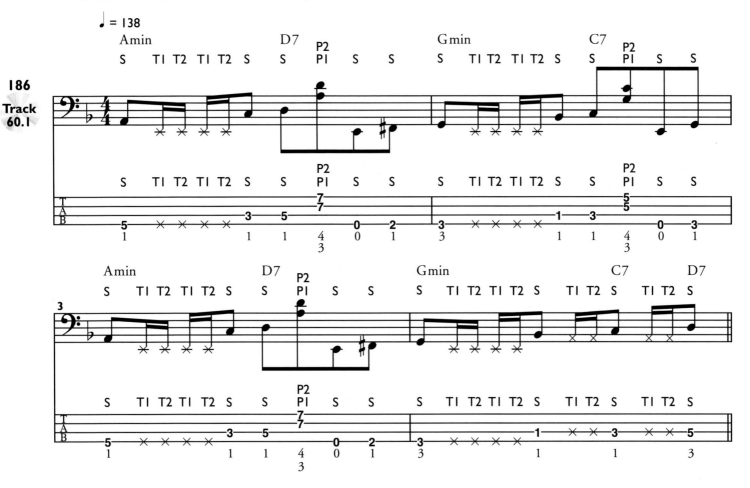

The dominant 7th groove below includes double thumping, hammer-ons, popped double stops, and slides.

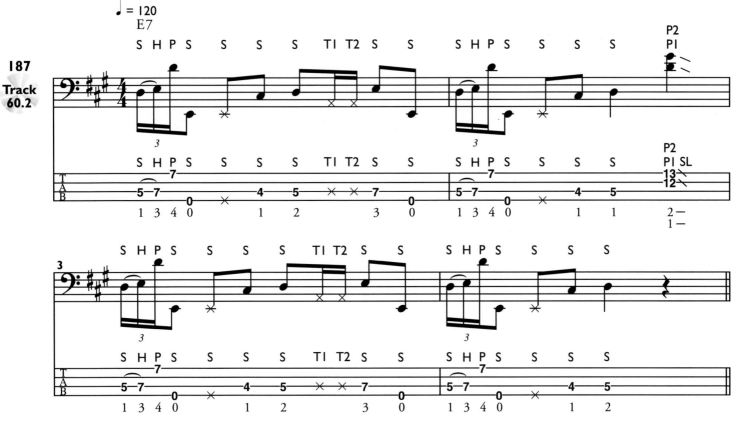

More Advanced Grooves

The following grooves use a combination of the various slap & pop techniques covered in this book. In many cases, if you don't yet have the double thumping technique mastered, you can use the slap technique instead; you just might not be able to play the groove as fast as the indicated tempo.

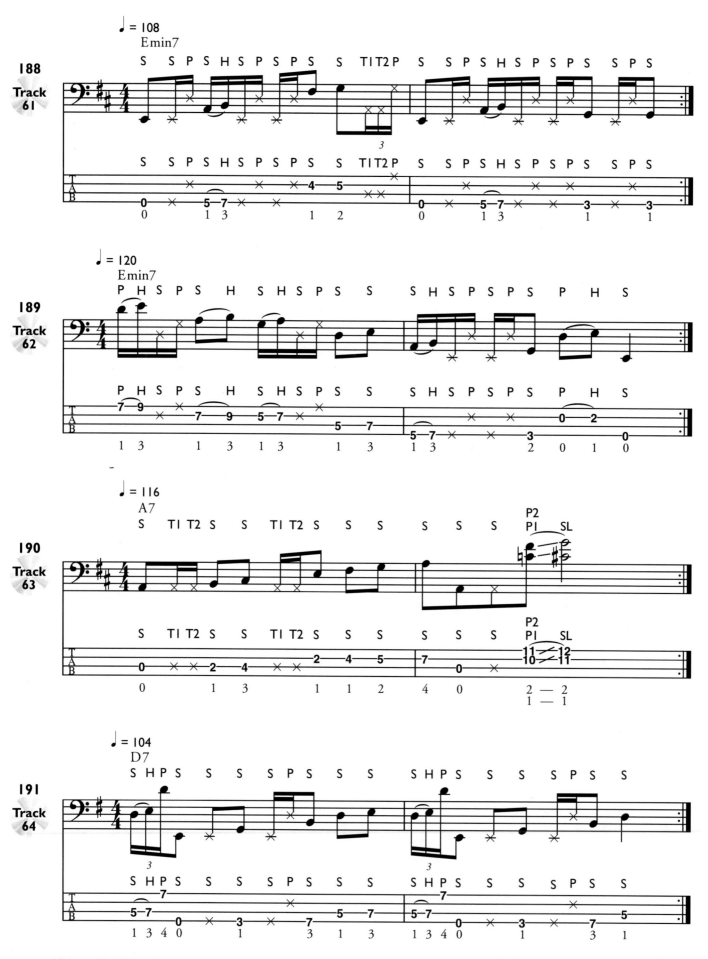

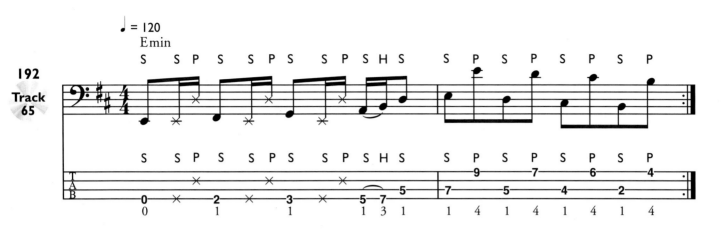

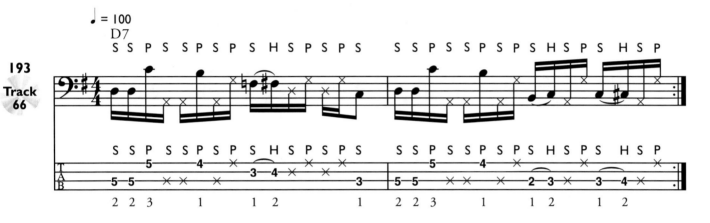

PHOTO BY JOE SIA/COURTESY OF STAR FILE PHOTO, INC.

Victor Wooten (b. 1964) is one of the foremost virtuoso bassists of his generation. Born into a musical family, he was playing gigs at age five with The Wooten Brothers Band. In 1988, he joined Béla Fleck and The Flecktones, along with his brother Roy "Future Man" Wooten. Victor soon became well known in the bass community for the ease with which he performed the intricate compositions of The Flecktones. The band's unique music defies classification, drawing from funk, bluegrass, and beyond. Wooten is widely regarded as a technical innovator who revolutionized the slap & pop technique.

We'll close out this chapter with a tune that features many of the techniques and concepts with which we have been working. The bass line was built using the E Minor Pentatonic scale and one note common to the E Natural Minor, E Harmonic Minor, and E Melodic Minor scales: F♯. As the title suggests, play the tune with a light touch; you'll be surprised how heavy it sounds!

Track 67 *Light Touch, Heavy Groove*

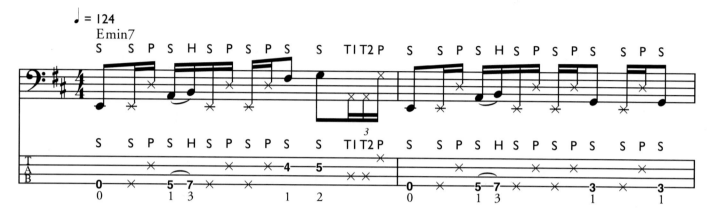

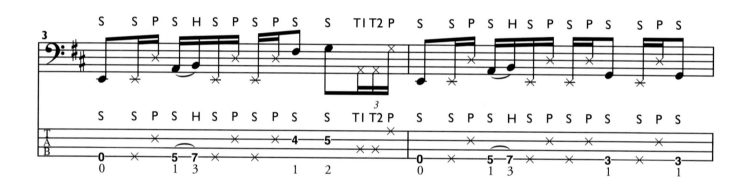

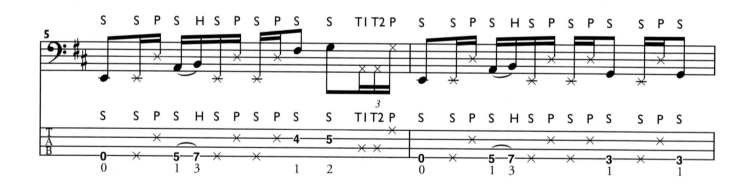

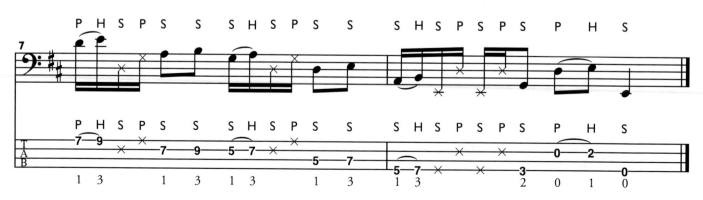

Chapter 12: Classic (and Soon to Be Classic) Funk Bass Grooves

Now that we have covered many funk bass techniques and played through lots of examples at a variety of ability levels, it's time to play some examples in the styles of funk classics we all know and love. We'll be using both the fingerstyle funk and slap & pop style for these grooves. Enjoy!

In the Style of "Brick House" by The Commodores

Here is another version of the groove, this time using the slap & pop style.

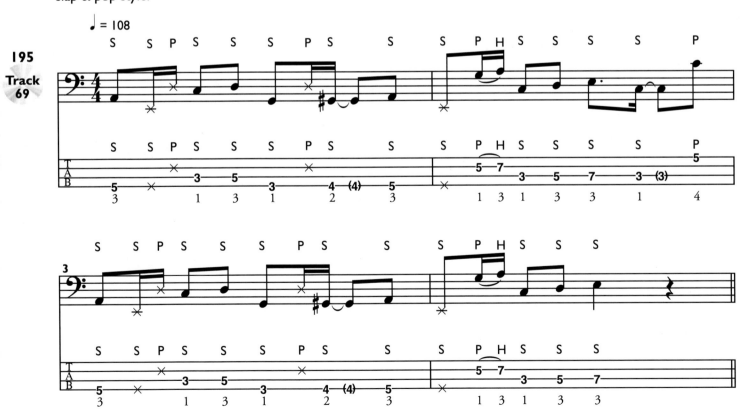

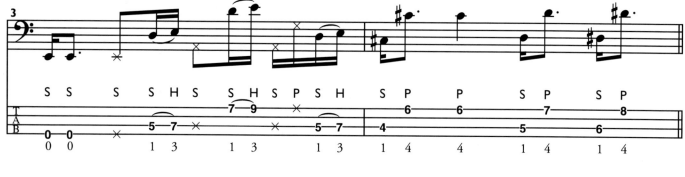

In the Style of "Superstition" by Stevie Wonder

In the Style of "Higher Ground" by Stevie Wonder

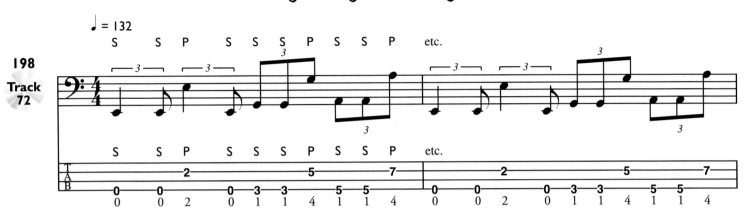

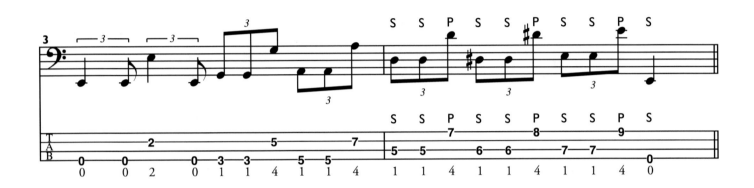

In the Style of "I Wish" by Stevie Wonder

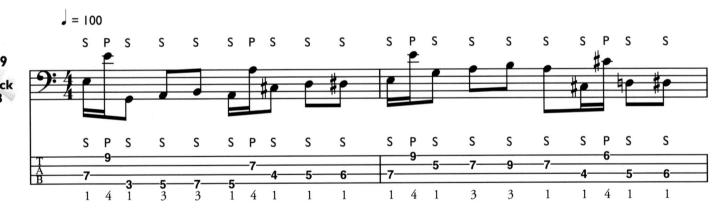

In the Style of "Cold Sweat" by James Brown

202
Track
76

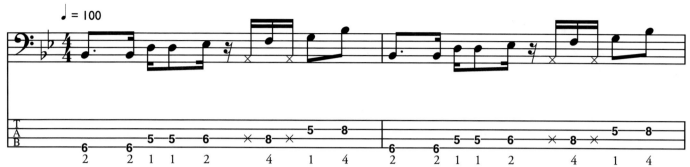

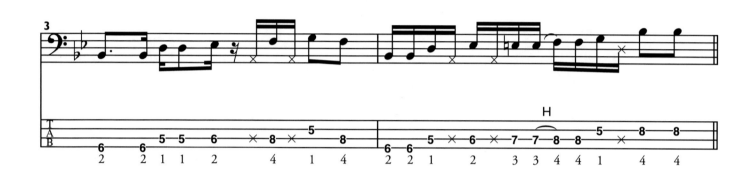

203
Track
77

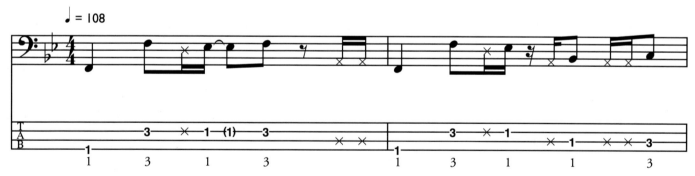

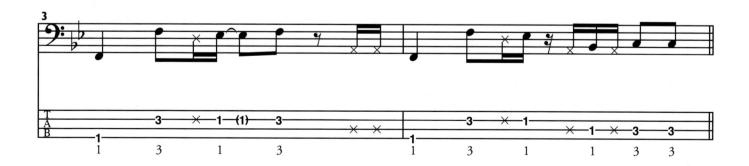

The slap & pop groove below is also in the style of "Chameleon."

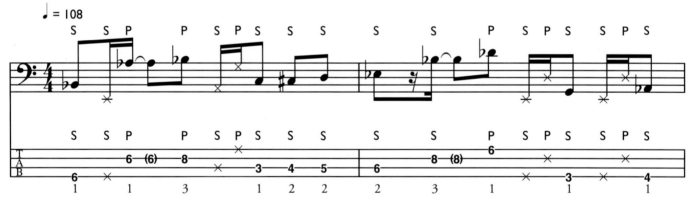

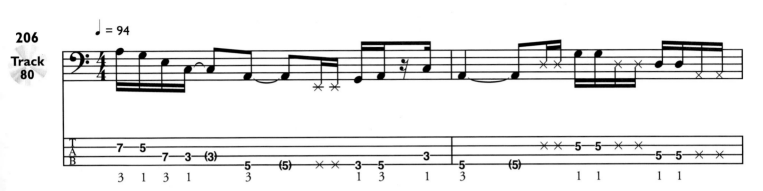

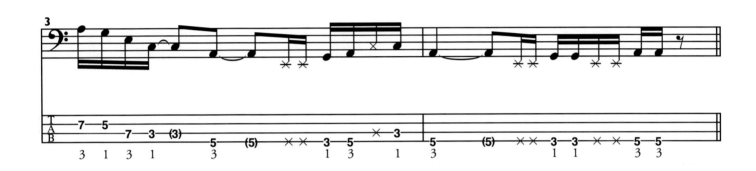

In the Style of "Sing a Simple Song" by The Meters

In the Style of "Express Yourself" by
Charles Wright & The Watts 103rd Street Rhythm Band

In the Style of "Low Rider" by War

In the Style of "Thank You (Falettinme Be Mice Elf Agin)" by Sly & the Family Stone

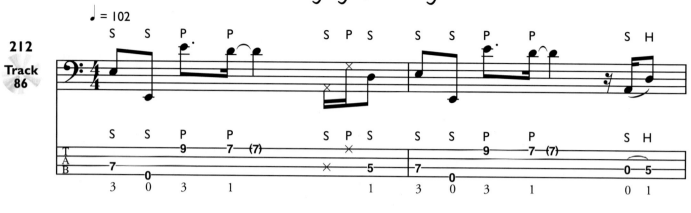

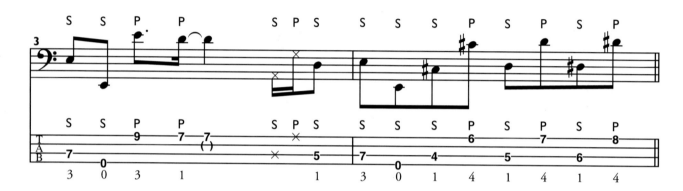

In the Style of "Slide" by Slave

In the Style of "Doing It to Death" by James Brown

214 Track 88

In the Style of "Fire" by The Ohio Players

215 Track 89

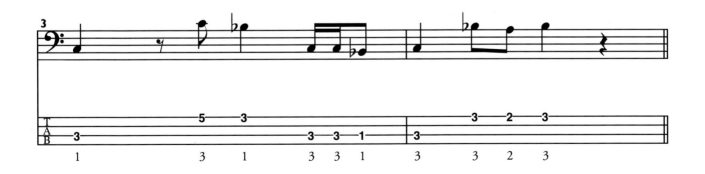

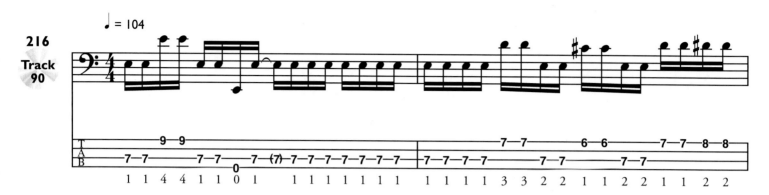

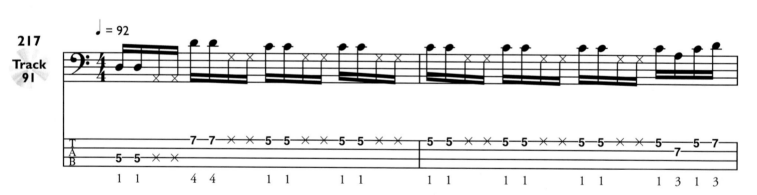

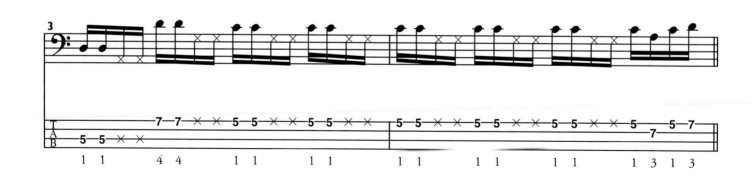

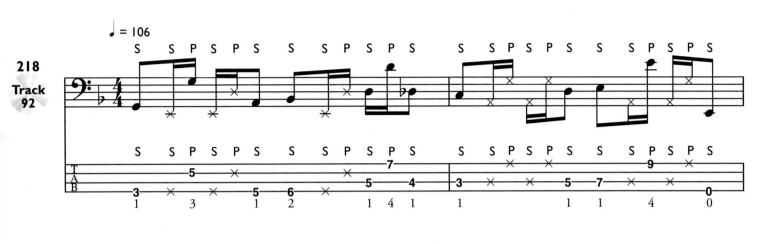

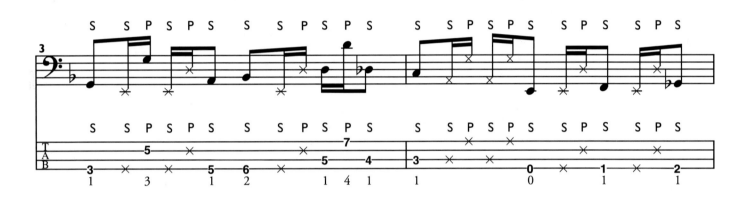

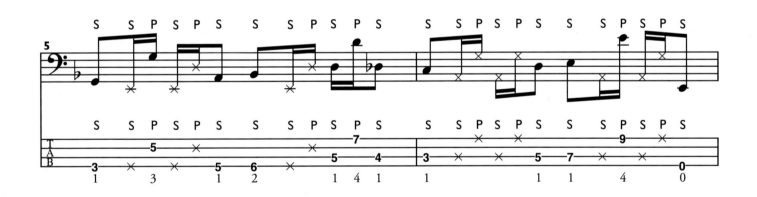

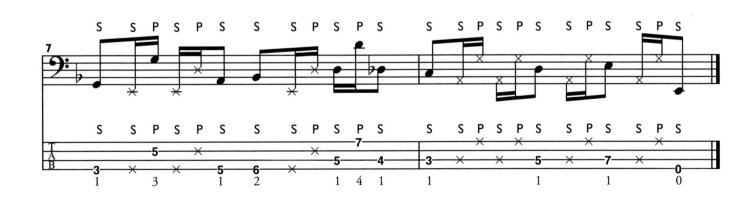

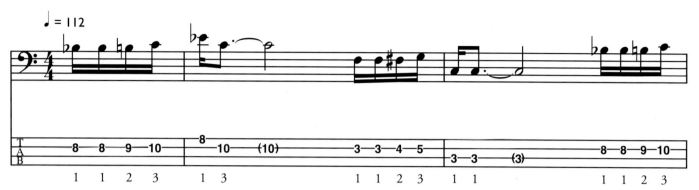

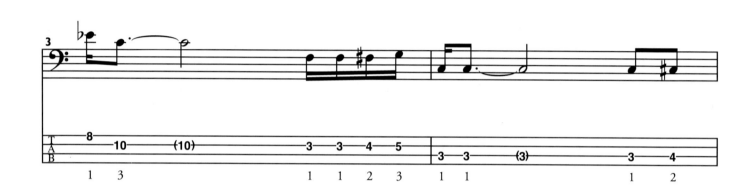

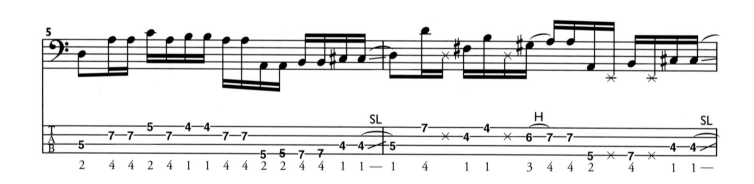

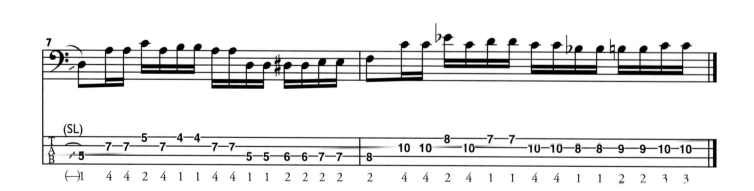

♩ = 116

220
Track 94

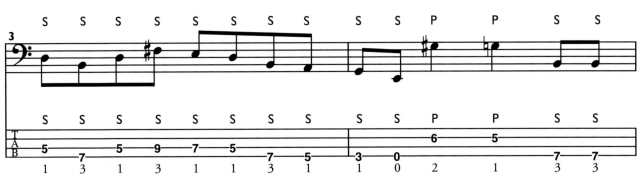

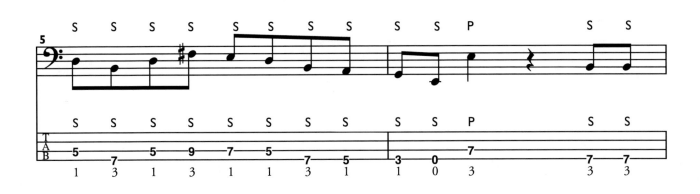

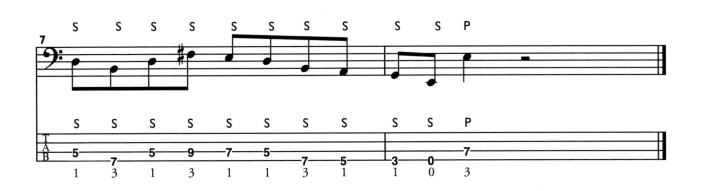

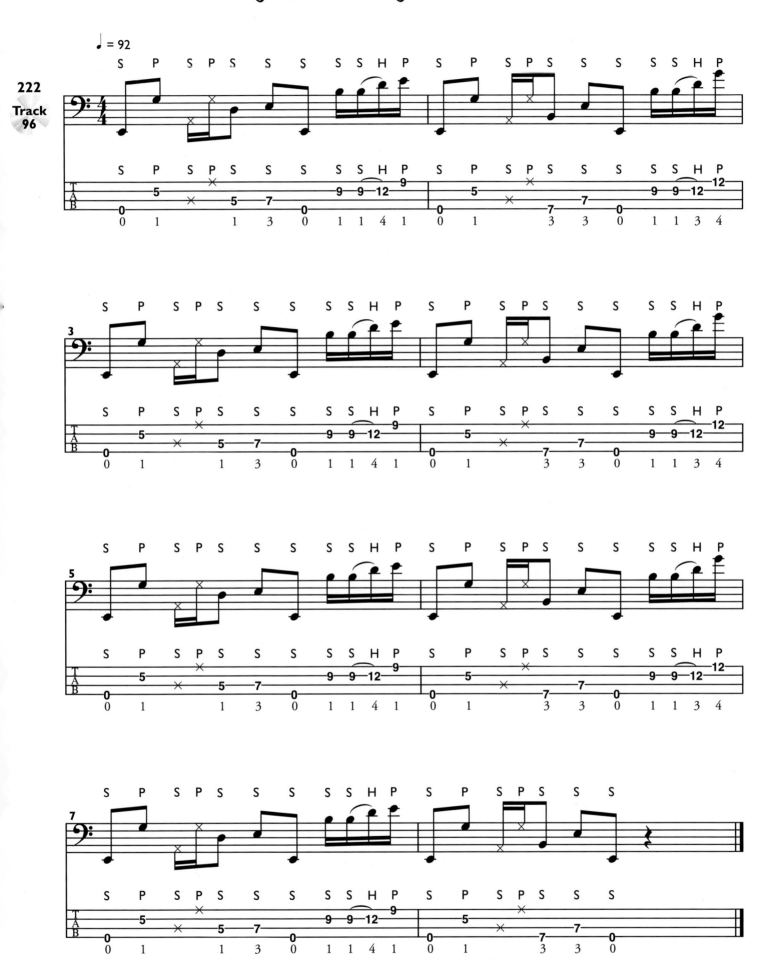

In the Style of "Sex in a Pan" by Béla Fleck and The Flecktones

Conclusion

You did it! You made it through a technically challenging, but hopefully rewarding, funk bass method. Although you have finished working through the book, you should check back periodically and retry examples that you found difficult to master. You can also try grooves at faster tempos to check on your progress.

Remember to always have fun and play music for the love of it. If you pursue the bass with love, dedication, and passion, any other rewards that may come your way, financial or otherwise, will just be icing on the cake.

It's important to listen to as many R&B, soul, and funk recordings as possible. There is no substitute for listening when learning a new genre of music. Also, try to figure out as many bass lines as you can from these recordings. Make them your own by applying the various techniques covered in this book.

Below, you will find a short list of important bassists. You should make a point of checking out as many of them as you can. A simple search on YouTube will bring up lots of cool videos of live performances that will blow your mind.

Good luck, have fun, and always remember to *make it funky!*

IMPORTANT FUNK BASSISTS	
Bassist	**Band**
Larry Graham	Sly & the Family Stone, Graham Central Station
Bootsy Collins	James Brown, Parliament-Funkadelic
James Jamerson	Motown/The Funk Brothers
Louis Johnson	The Brothers Johnson
Verdine White	Earth, Wind & Fire
Stanley Clarke	Return to Forever, Jeff Beck, solo
Jaco Pastorius	Weather Report, Pat Metheny, solo
Marcus Miller	Miles Davis, David Sanborn, solo
Rocco Prestia	Tower of Power
Gary Willis	Tribal Tech, Allan Holdsworth
George Porter, Jr.	The Meters
Les Claypool	Primus, Oysterhead
Flea	The Red Hot Chili Peppers
Mark King	Level 42, solo
Darryl Jones	Miles Davis, Sting, The Rolling Stones
Victor Wooten	Béla Fleck and The Flecktones, solo